THE H SENSITIVE ATHLETE

MW00952766

How to Embody
The Magic of Your True Self
In & Out of Sport

MADELINE BARLOW, PhD

Self -n- DAYS
Publish 30
This Is The Year For
Your New Book

WWW.SELFPUBLISHN30DAYS.COM

Published by *Self Publish -N- 30 Days*

Copyright 2021 Madeline Barlow, PhD

Printed in the United States of America

ISBN: 979-8-45950-489-7

1. Nonfiction 2. Self-Help 3. Sports & Recreation

Madeline Barlow, PhD *The Highly Sensitive Athlete: How to Embody The Magic of Your True Self In & Out of Sport*

Disclaimer/Warning:

ACKNOWLEDGMENTS

Writing my book and co-authoring another by my 30th birthday is something I never even imagined I'd do—but here I am! First things first, I want to acknowledge the people in my life who have inspired me to write this particular book.

Thank you to the hundreds of student-athletes and coaches I've worked with who have trusted me enough to show me their sensitive souls in our sessions. Your courage to be yourself has helped me do the same in writing this book and sharing my story with the world. I've always dreamed of writing a book, but I never knew what to write about. Thank you for the push in the right direction.

To the many teachers and guides along the way who provided me with the knowledge and skills to write this book from start to finish—in particular, thank you to Dr. Michael Sachs, Dr. Lois Butcher-Poffley, Dr. Bryan Myers, and my personal editing assistant, my mom, Marlene. To my family as a whole, for supporting me in more ways than one, thank you.

Finally, I would like to do a personal shoutout to Taj Dashaun and the team at Self Publish-N-30 Days for guidance and support throughout the writing process. You've made writing this book a seamless process from start to finish, and I'm incredibly grateful to have connected with you in divine timing.

TABLE OF CONTENTS

PREFACE:

AN OPEN LETTER TO MY 18-YEAR-OLD SELF

Hey Mads,

It's me, Madeline. You're 30 now. I remember all of the things you wanted to do before 30—the things you were so sure about. Marriage, having children, being completely settled.

Well, I'll tell you what. You are closing in on the third thing, although it's more of an internal feeling of "settled." Actually, it's this feeling of being whole. You don't need anyone or anything to "complete" you or make you feel valid. Your value is determined from the inside out.

Between you and me, this journey to self-acceptance and self-love hasn't been easy. On the outside, you did everything you could to be positive, generous, and caring, but on the inside? You were hurting. Since you were in elementary school, all you ever wanted was to be liked, accepted, and understood. Now, at 30 years old, you've come to recognize that you can love and accept all parts of yourself!

I wanted to write this letter to understand our journey a bit more from my perspective. You know what they say. Hindsight is 20/20. It's also my hope that you learn to keep your heart wide-open as you go through the next four years. Yet, that's never really been a problem for you, has it?

At 18, you went into college so open, carefree, and with so much love in your heart. That love radiated towards the people around you (just like in high school) and especially towards swimming.

Man, did you love to swim. One thing was missing, however. While you set out to please everyone around you because you wanted to fit in and avoid rejection, you never paused to realize you were inadvertently rejecting yourself—your true, authentic Self.

You thought you had lost yourself along the way. But your true Self was there all along, just covered up, afraid to stand out, and ready to shine. I'm so sorry you felt like you were a screw-up (FYI, you're not) and should have it all figured out (FYI, no one has it all figured out). You did the best you could with what you knew.

So, if I could tell you one thing, it would be to pause. Go inward. Listen. This inner wisdom is all you need to uncover your true Self, the unapologetic version of Madeline. By the way, this version of Madeline is so freaking confident!

When you align with the true you, you will understand why time flies because you will live in the present moment and will be sensitized to your life (which is painful at times, not going to lie).

You will recognize that your true strength lies in your sensitivity and your ability to connect with yourself and others, especially when they need it most. This superpower will be waiting for you whenever you're ready to claim it as yours!

I know you love to swim, and your heart will break when you swim your final butterfly race. You are meant to fly in this life, just maybe not in the way you always thought.

I love you, and I see you. Be brave. Be strong and sensitive. I'll be here when you're ready for your journey back home to the truest, most sensitive you!

Love always and forever,
Madeline

INTRODUCTION:

WHY THIS BOOK

I wrote this book not only because of my personal experience being a Highly Sensitive Person (HSP) and athlete but because of the Highly Sensitive Athletes (HSAs). Highly sensitive athletes have and continue to reach out to me for guidance and support. It only takes one session for me to observe their sensitive qualities, while it may take a few weeks, months, or even years for a highly sensitive athlete to recognize and accept this trait within themselves. I wrote this book so anyone labeled as "too sensitive" can take back the power of being their true Self.

Author's note: *Over the last several years, I have come home to my true Self. Note the capitalization of "S" in Self; it signifies your Higher Self. If you have a dedicated spiritual practice, you may have heard this term before. Your Higher Self can be equated to the wise being who is your real Self. The Self is the energy of your highest potential waiting to be expressed, free of conditioning.*

My life changed the moment I chose to look inward and lean into my sensitive nature. You deserve that same chance. No one has written about the highly sensitive athlete, and I feel this is because being sensitive in sport is not valued as much as its counterpart. By raising awareness of what it means to be sensitive and how you can use this trait to your advantage, I hope that you, as a highly sensitive athlete, will have the athletic experience of your dreams and beyond.

Who Is This Book For?

This book is for you if you are a current or former athlete and resonate with being highly sensitive. Others may have called you "too sensitive" or have told you to "stop being so emotional." This book is for you if you are exhausted from covering up your true Self to "fit in" to sport culture and if you are ready to expand and align with your potential in sport and life outside of sport.

This book is also for you if you are a coach or sport administrator. You will gain a deeper awareness and understanding of many of your athletes. You will learn how best to motivate and validate the experience of your highly sensitive athletes, enhancing those relationships, and, in turn, generating peak performance. Parents of a highly sensitive athlete will also benefit from this book. Awareness of what it means to be sensitive in sport and life will influence your relationship with your child on a deeper level.

Performers outside of sports can also benefit from what is inside these pages. Those in graduate school, in the high-pressure corporate world, or artists, such as musicians, actors, DJs, music producers, and professional dancers, will also benefit from a genuine understanding of what it means to be highly sensitive as it relates to their experiences. I will mainly refer to athletes and former athletes, as this is my area of expertise, but please know you can replace "athlete" with your personal identity as a performer or high achiever.

When to Use this Book?

This book will benefit you at all stages of your athletic experience and beyond. There is a section specific to current athletes and using your sensitivities as a superpower while competing. This book would be helpful to high-school, college-aged, and professional athletes.

Additionally, this book is meant for athletes who have since transitioned out of sport and performance, having moved on to the next stage of life. Two parts of this book are devoted to navigating the transition itself and aligning with your sensitivity after sport.

Overall, there is no wrong time to pick up this book. Most likely, it will *find you* at the time you most need it, just like Elaine Aron's book, *The Highly Sensitive Person*, found me in a meta-physical shop I stumbled upon several years ago.

How to Use It

So, you align with being highly sensitive and are an athlete, former athlete, coach, parent, or performer. Now what? In the final part of this book, I hone in on embodying your sensitive traits.

I include embodiment activities for you to put into practice. At a certain point, awareness will only get you so far. Just like it takes showing up to your sport's training daily to progress in skill and performance, it is the habit of stepping into your true Self that will lead to transformation.

When you reach Chapter 10, "Embodying the Magic of Your True Self," it is crucial to recognize that you are not alone. If, at any time, you feel called to reach out for support, follow your intuition. Whether you connect with another practitioner or me, asking for help is the strongest step you can take towards embodying your true, sensitive Self. I have personally had support for the last three years, and I am forever grateful.

Finally, take note of your progress from start to finish of this book. Use the space below to write down how you are feeling at this moment and consider these questions:

In this moment, do you perceive yourself as sensitive?

_____

Do you view sensitivity as positive or negative?

_____

Do you feel your sensitivity is valued in your sport environment or by others in your life?

_____

_____

_____

_____

_____

List any emotions or experiences you have had regarding being sensitive in sport and life.

_____

_____

_____

_____

_____

As you move through the sections of this book, reflect on your starting point. Share your progress with someone you care about. Just like you set and share goals in your sport, it's important to share the steps of your journey with someone with whom you connect on a deeper level.

I'm thrilled to walk this path with you. First, I would like to share more about my experience as a highly sensitive athlete and why it's vital for me to share this book with you.

CHAPTER 1:

MY STORY AS AN ATHLETE & HIGHLY SENSITIVE PERSON

A s a former collegiate athlete and highly sensitive person, it is a thrill of my first 30 trips around the sun to shed light on both topics. Let's take a trip back in time so you can envision the path that led me to write this book.

For most of my childhood, I grew up in the pool. Whether I was down the shore at the neighborhood pool or a few miles from home at another pool I called home every summer for a quarter of a century, I adored the water. It was my safe space, which was something I realized and appreciated even more upon recognizing my sensitive nature. The water was the most supportive thing in my life besides my family.

I loved to swim, and the pool seemed to love me back, providing me with the most beautiful experiences. When I was eight years old, I joined the swim team after the head coach saw me at swim lesson trials. He called my home that night and asked my mom if I'd like to be on the team. I remember being so excited.

That was only the beginning. For the next few years, swim practice was my favorite part of the day. While I enjoyed school and was the third-grader who jumped off the bus and sat right down to do her homework, nothing brought me as much joy as swimming did. I was in my element.

As far as I can remember, swimming (when I was younger) was something I did for *me*. I was racing against myself and the clock. I had no reason to doubt myself and swam best times pretty consistently. My abilities made me feel special and unique.

Swimming was the only sport I participated in. By the time I was 12, I had developed an athlete identity (more on this in "I Am an Athlete."). Whenever we had to do "ice breakers" on the first day of school, my go-to was, "My name is Madeline, and I'm a swimmer." I was proud of my identity as a swimmer! I talked about it whenever given the opportunity and with whoever would listen. I was head over heels for the sport.

Fast forward to eighth grade—things began to change, mentally and physically. The summer beforehand, I went from a size 0 in jeans to a size 6. It was a bit of a shock, to say the least. Somewhere along the line, I ended up with a botched haircut, leading to some serious feelings of embarrassment.

At one point, I was wearing the same black and orange swim team sweatshirt several times a week, feeling uncomfortable in my changing body. I was made fun of by a boy on my team for the blackheads on my nose. My grades began to suffer for the first time in my life. Math class felt nearly impossible, so I ended up with a tutor. I couldn't wrap my head around the information—it was overwhelming.

While I didn't know it at the time, this was when I first started covering up my true Self and hid from the world. I felt things **so deeply** and didn't know what to do with my emotions other than pushing them down and keeping them hidden from the world. Can you relate? You will learn more about this in chapter four, "Why So Sensitive?"

As time passed, swimming and school became more difficult, yet I made it work. I suppose this is why no one realized I was struggling. Gone were the days of swimming the best time every weekend or getting a perfect score on every assignment. I went from feeling special to feeling ashamed. I always valued telling the truth, yet I found myself hiding test scores from my parents at times. I couldn't admit that I wasn't perfect in school or the pool.

When it came time for college, I chose to go to a school just over two hours away from home where I already knew a few people from swimming over the years. I was scared to go somewhere totally unknown. Still, I was excited about college, especially swimming, as I had reached peak performance by the end of my senior year.

In the pool, I felt on top of the world! Nothing could bring me down, or so I thought. For whatever reason, I expected to have deep and meaningful friendships in college, just like I had on my high school club swim team. We were genuinely a family in all the best ways. I could confide in just about anyone on my team, so I figured the same when I entered my freshman year of college. I was wrong.

My naivete got the best of me. My lack of awareness even more so. Yet, every year, I hoped for the best. I so desperately wanted to connect with my teammates on a soul level that I put on mask upon mask to fit in. I covered up my true, sensitive Self. Although, if this 'covering up' had indeed occurred, why then did I find myself exploding with emotion time and time again? We'll dive into this later in this book.

To bring my story in sport to a close, let's zone in on the end. As I mentioned above, swimming was my first love. It brought immense joy and deep pain. I only recently recognized that swimming and the pool did not cause the pain. Rather, the pain was self-inflicted.

Year after year, I gave away my power to those around me. I allowed myself to be hurt again and again, which translated to how I viewed the world, including my perception of the sport itself.

The moment I touched the wall of what became my final 100-butterfly of my swimming career, I felt unexplainable pain and loss. The sorrow reached deep in my soul as if a piece of me had died and left my body. I know now this was the start of my "unmasking." I was finally able to express my true Self, but this meant feeling it **all**. I thought I had to release my athlete identity and the love I carried for the sport of swimming. I had to say goodbye.

Moving on didn't seem so hard at first, as I went directly into my master's program, which took me to Wilmington, North Carolina. It was my first time far away from home, college, old teammates, and swimming itself. The separation came as a relief. The downside? I never honestly dealt with this loss, the death of myself as an "athlete." I just chose to push through to a new identity as a "graduate student."

I continued to cover up my pain by drinking excessively on the weekends. Spending way too much money on a personal trainer to stay in shape, I distracted myself from my emotions by having the TV on a constant loop. Quiet and stillness were not an option.

This lifestyle continued through my time in North Carolina and into my trip home to Philadelphia, where I started a doctoral program in the Psychology of Human Movement. My specialty? Sport psychology. My soul longed to guide and support athletes. I wanted to become the person I wish I had when I was competing.

I know what you're thinking. "Now was the time Madeline took off the mask and aligned with her sensitive Self." Nope. I would argue I put on a new mask. I made it to this level, a high achiever. I had to have it all together. But inside? My anxiety was at its peak. My sensitivities eventually found their way out, typically if I drank too much or after leading a discussion group or giving a presentation. I would feel ill with a raging headache and sometimes an upset stomach. My body was tired of hiding its actual needs.

In the final year of my doctoral program, my body had had enough. I worked with athletes at a Division I university on top of finishing my dissertation. The next thing I knew, I found myself walking to the ER with chest pains. Chest pains? Fourteen years of swimming, and I had never felt anything like this. Yet, after five hours in the ER, my tests came back normal. Physically, I was 'fine,' but I knew, with all my being, I was not fine.

All of this led me to the turning point of my journey towards uncovering my true Self. I began going to weekly acupuncture, tried yoga, and explored Reiki (also known as energy healing). These holistic modalities provided me with the awareness and validation I was looking for.

My sensitive soul was in shambles. I covered up my sensitivity to my pain, the feelings of others, and stimulation from my environment. My true Self desired to be expressed, and it had no other choice but to show up as physical pain to get my attention.

Finally, I was listening. My journey from there on out was centered around accepting my sensitivity to align with my true Self. The more I stepped into align-ment, the better I felt. My anxiety subsided, which made space for confidence. I shed my physical pain and physical weight (that I had carried for years following the end of swimming).

I now use my keen observation skills, attention to detail, and understanding of the emotions of others in my work with current and former athletes. Interestingly enough, the majority of athletes who walk through my door share these qualities. It's my greatest privilege to help them tune in to their own gifts and bear witness to the "aha" moments and watch them begin using their sensitive qualities to their advantage.

You, highly sensitive athletes, are my inspiration for writing this book, as I know there are many more out there who have been hiding for too long. I hope that, through awareness and application of the right tools, you will be able to step into your power—the power and *magic* of embodying your true, sensitive Self, in **and** out of sport.

CHAPTER 2:

BEING SENSITIVE IN A SUPERCHARGED WORLD

W hen I use the word sensitive, many people cringe or recommend that I use a different word. For this book, I am choosing to shine a light on what it means to be sensitive to help you release any stigma or negative stories you hold.

Why? Because this stigma is a social construct. The word (sensitive) itself means nothing without the perception people place upon it. Let's take back the power with a positive connotation of sensitivity. It no longer has to be a misunderstood trait. Statements like, "Stop being so sensitive" will no longer bring up feelings of shame. It's essential to let go of shame to make room for stepping into your sensitivity.

A majority of the athletes with whom I work identify themselves as highly sensitive. They typically feel alone in this, but I'm here to show you that you are, in fact, amongst many other sensitive athletes, myself included. To be sensitive is to feel more, see more, understand more, hear more, and be aware of more. Yes, it has the potential to be overwhelming, but only if you give it the chance. Throughout this book, you will learn how to transform your sensitivity into your strength.

The world we live in is supercharged. Especially on the east coast of the United States, where I've lived most of my life, the city of Philadelphia itself is fast-paced. On the street, move out of the way if you aren't walking four miles per hour at least! Many people have their heads down, avoiding eye contact, as they have places to be, things to do.

When I moved to Philly, I had yet to uncover my sensitive Self and was surprised to find that I was exhausted every single day. It wasn't until three years into living there that I came across the book, *The Highly Sensitive Person* by Elaine Aron. I picked it up at a cute boutique, read the back, and checked off "yes" to every question. It was mind-blowing! I listed them below so that you can do the same.

"Is this you?

- *Are you easily overwhelmed by bright lights, strong smells, sirens, harsh fabrics?*
- *Do you get worked up when you have a lot to do in a short amount of time?*
- *Do you avoid violent movies or TV shows (or fast forward/cover your eyes through the violent scenes)?*
- *Do you need alone time following a busy day or have to leave the party the moment you notice your social meter hits empty?*
- *Do you make it a point to avoid overwhelming or upsetting situations?*
- *Do you notice or enjoy the depth of music you listen to, the food you eat, or other works of art?*
- *Do you have a vivid inner world and imagination?*
- *Were you ever perceived as sensitive or shy as a child (by parents, teachers, coaches, friends, et cetera)?"*

First and foremost, please know you are not alone, and being an HSP is a normal trait. While being sensitive may not be highly regarded in our society and sport specifically, I invite you to view this trait as an innate gift.

You navigate this supercharged world in a different way than many. By the way, 15 to 20% of the population carries the HSP trait. By leaning in, you can use it to your advantage in sport and life.

It is important to recognize your sensitivity and learn how to navigate your unique experience of the world as HSPs have reported higher levels of stress and more frequent bouts of illness or physical symptoms (similar to my chest pains above). Those who are highly sensitive can be more in tune with their body and mind, which may result in noticing symptoms or feeling pain others may not, including the experience of stress and anxiety.

If you still aren't sure if you are an HSP, scan the code to take the HSP Quiz. The higher the score, the more highly sensitive you are. A score of 14 qualifies as highly sensitive. I scored 26, if that tells you anything about my sensitivity! What's your score?

HSP Quiz QR code:

Common Perceptions of Specific Personality Types

Another important aspect I want to shed light on is the perception of personality types or specific traits related to sport culture. As the focus of this book is on being highly sensitive, we'll start there.

Highly Sensitive vs. Hypersensitive

When I say "sensitive," what is the first thought that comes to mind? For many, they typically say sensitive means emotional. If this was your impression until now, you aren't alone or wrong, but it isn't the complete picture.

You are thinking of "hypersensitivity," which involves a lack of emotional resilience, often leading to an extreme emotional reaction. People who experience emotional hypersensitivity haven't learned healthy coping mechanisms to manage their emotions. Unmanaged hypersensitivity may result in viewing a dropped ball during a lacrosse game as profoundly shameful and embarrassing; this person might begin weeping, yelling, or throw their stick.

Or, to stick with the swimming examples, an athlete may touch the wall, look up at the scoreboard, register the less-than-stellar time in their head, and rage out. I've seen countless swimmers smack the water (out of anger rather than excitement) and proceed to throw their racing goggles at the **concrete** wall. Yikes!

Author's note: *I never have and never will throw a pair of goggles at a wall. My goggles were valuable cargo and had to remain in pristine condition. You can't see the wall with a pair of severely scraped-up goggles!*

On the other hand, being **highly** sensitive means to feel more deeply, hear, see, understand, and live more deeply. If you're reading this book, either you or someone you know is highly sensitive. Do you notice the finest of details from a conversation you had two years ago, or are you able to pull out the spelling mistakes from a book you are reading (professionals edited it, yet you found that *one* mistake)? Do you listen to music and feel **deeply** moved by the lyrics or the melody, to the point where some songs make your eyes fill with tears? These are aspects of the highly sensitive trait (see the above list or hsperson.com for more information).

As you can probably now tell, to be sensitive is not simply being "emotional." As a highly sensitive person, you are uniquely *perceptive.* There is power in understanding the actual definition of being highly sensitive, allowing you to recognize and celebrate who you are and how you're meant to show up in this world.

A highly sensitive person who has yet to recognize this trait within themselves and hasn't learned how to cope with their sensitivity to overstimulation may experience hypersensitive, emotional reactions. If you feel as though you are like this, I have also chosen to write this book to teach *you* the tools you need to navigate the potential challenges of being a highly sensitive person in and out of sport. It's a gift, not a curse, but only if you learn to acknowledge and accept who you truly are! This awareness will allow you to take action and begin living the life you desire.

Extroversion vs. Introversion vs. Shyness
Another quality that is essential to understand is the difference between extroversion, introversion, and shyness. Most people assume extroversion equals

outgoing, while introversion is equivalent to shyness. While an extroverted person may appear more willing to socialize, these personality traits actually have less to do with how you present to the world and more about how you **recharge** your energy.

For example, I am introverted by nature, and I now recognize that I need alone time to recharge my battery. I do *not* gain energy while surrounded by people, regardless of how much I like or feel connected to said people. Being an introvert is even more relevant to my trait as an HSP.

I cannot stress this enough. If you are introverted *and* highly sensitive and don't want to burn out, make alone time a priority. It's essential to your well-being and effectiveness in society (however you choose to enter society through work and life, that is).

Also, please note that introverts are not necessarily shy. Shyness stands on its own. When I'm around *my* people, I am the farthest thing from shy. Put me in a room where I feel uncomfortable, however, and you'll catch me in the corner petting the dog and eating snacks all night.

On the other end of the spectrum, there are those individuals who are extroverted. Again, this is related to how they recharge their battery. You will find those who are extroverted recharge in the presence of others, whether it is going out shopping, having another hang out at the park, or at the dinner table with family.

They are typically the 'yes!' people—those who are always down for going out and doing all the things. After several hours of socializing, the last thing on my mind is family dinner, if I'm completely honest. I need my bed or bath, pajamas, and a good Netflix binge or my favorite book, but to each their own.

Introverts are extremely misunderstood in sport and are often viewed negatively for being more independent or needing space from their team. This book intends to bring light to the individual differences present amongst athletes (and former athletes) to allow for deeper understanding and more meaningful connections between athletes and their coaches, teammates, and family members.

CHAPTER 3:

"I AM AN ATHLETE."

I f you're reading this book, you identified with being an athlete (or performer) at one point or another. I would bet you've said things like, "[insert sport here] is my life," "I can't, I have practice," or "I am a [insert sport identity here]." I have said all of the above throughout my 14 years as a competitive swimmer.

I went to school, did my homework, swam, went to sleep, and repeat (with some food in between). On the weekends, I usually had swim meets anywhere from several hours to three days. Swimming truly was my life.

What is an Athletic Identity?

It's not surprising to learn that I had developed what is referred to as "athletic identity," or the extent to which one identifies with the athlete role. I lived and breathed my sport, chlorine fumes and all. Hindsight is 20/20, they say, and I didn't know anything about this until I started my doctoral studies.

The following few sections are based on three years of research on athletic identity and the transition out of sport. I had the opportunity to deeply investigate something that continues to influence my life several years out of swimming. I am so grateful for the experience (thank you, Dr. Sachs and Dr. B), and I believe this research will help you gain awareness of your own experience in and out of sport.

How much do you or did you identify with being an athlete? The Athletic Identity Measurement Scale (AIMS) is widely used in research to measure athletic identity, but let's keep it simple for this book. On a scale of 1 to 10, how much do you identify with the role of "athlete?"

If you have since retired from competitive sport, think back to a time when you were heavily involved in your sport. Does the number differ between then and now? When did you notice a change? Make a note of this below.

Then ⟶ **Now**

Positive and Negative Influences of AI

Both the positive and negative influences of holding a strong and exclusive athletic identity are that a higher number on the scale is associated with feeling connected to the sole social role of "athlete." For example, I perceived my identity as a "swimmer," and I did not share this distinction with other roles such as "student," "daughter," or "musician."

While I was *all* of these things when I was swimming, I never put much weight into other identities outside of the pool.

Have you done the same? The positive effects of a strong and exclusive athletic identity are the development of a secure sense of Self and enhanced athletic performance. The same level of sport performance is less likely to occur if you hold multiple strong identities or social roles.

This is why you see many athletes choose to specialize in a sport at some point in their athletic careers. Sport participation also plays a role in positive youth development and influencing development components such as structure, supportive relationships, opportunities to belong, skill-building, and positive social norms. This enhanced self-perception is a clear sense of Self characterized by high self-awareness and a clear purpose in life.

On the other hand, an exclusive athletic identity can lead to mental health challenges when an individual suffers an injury or is cut from the team. This is typically due to the individual's strong sense of athletic identity. They are less likely to explore other potential career or educational endeavors because of their high sport involvement levels.

When an individual experiences identity foreclosure, the closing off of oneself from exploring multiple identities or ideologies at an early age, the individual is more likely to experience psychological and behavioral discomfort. This discomfort comes when faced with transitioning out of one's sport or forced into 'retirement' (like being cut from a team or suffering a career-ending injury).

Certainly, some student-athletes retire from their respective sport and feel a sense of relief and adjust well to their life without it. On the other hand, many individuals encounter a period of maladjustment due to identity issues, lack of coping processes, support, and career planning. Research has demonstrated that individuals with a strong and exclusive athletic identity are less likely to develop coping mechanisms for retirement as they experience anxiety when faced with the prospect of life after sport.

Leaving Room for Other Roles and Interests

Based on research, including the findings of my doctoral dissertation, it's clear that athletes would benefit from creating space in their lives to explore interests outside of sport. As mentioned above, having a strong, exclusive athletic identity leads to better performance, but at what cost?

You miss out on connecting with friends, trying on other hats, liking some things, and disliking others. Simply put, you may miss out on being a kid.

When I found the time to **slow down** and look back at my experience as an athlete, I was surprised by what I saw.

I saw a sensitive, intuitive child who truly loved the water. I also saw a young girl who was fearful of trying new things and extremely sensitive to rejection and failure. She played the piano for seven years but quit before eighth grade and used swimming as an excuse.

I remember the real reason was my building frustration every time I sat down to practice and failed to play the song perfectly. Playing the piano, and playing it well, meant more eyes on me. I can feel the heat on my face as I conjure up this memory.

Swimming was different. While I may have had eyes on me during a race, my eyes and ears were underwater—the cheers muffled, the faces blurred. I was safe from any judgment—until I jumped out of the pool, at least. After a race, the locker room became my safe haven.

I tried a few other things as a child. I went to tennis camp, golf camp, played the clarinet for two years, and was a choir member. None of them stuck like swimming. On the one hand, swimming **lit me up**! I loved it.

I loved to play the piano, too. So, why did I quit? My sensitivity got the best of me, so I chose to commit to the place I felt most comfortable—face in the water, staring at the black line. It became the most constant thing in my life.

It didn't take long until swimming was the center of my universe. All my friends were on my team (with only a few exceptions). I missed birthday parties and hangouts on the weekend, and swimming was my favorite topic to talk about. It was my entire identity.

Many athletes resonate with this story. This is why it is essential to help current athletes expand their perspective or "widen the blinders" to not miss out on the beauty all around them.

You may ask, "but if 100% of my energy and attention isn't on my sport, how will I reach my goals?" By creating space for *more* beauty and *more* joy, you are better able to be effective and in the zone at practice or during a game—when it counts most. When you **feel good**, and your internal drive or fire is **lit**, you perform well, too. By making space to do more of what lights you up, you will notice a shift, both internally and externally.

When you take part in an activity, whether it's your sport or something else, notice how you *feel*. You can do this regarding the people you surround yourself with, as well. How can you bring more of these feel-good activities into your life?

As a former athlete, you may still wear these blinders, only noticing what's right in front of you, like your current job or monotonous routine. I invite you to pause now and make a list of anything and everything that brings you **joy**!

What interests you? What activities do you like simply because they are **fun** or make you feel **good** (versus activities where you are focused on the outcome)?

Here's a look at my list of joyful self-care activities:

- Walking outside
- Taking a bath
- Meditating
- Baking cookies
- Dancing and listening to music
- Reading & writing
- Connecting with other people with similar interests
- Traveling the world and learning about other people's culture
- Watching cooking shows and eating food I love
- Relaxing at home with a cup of tea

Your turn!

- _____
- _____
- _____
- _____
- _____
- _____
- _____
- _____
- _____
- _____
- _____
- _____

If this is your first time making self-care a priority, that's okay! I commend you for taking this critical step—no need to dive in head-first and do everything. After making your list, pick three that stand out to you or excite you most. For the next two weeks, make the time for the three you selected.

You don't need to do all three every single day. Instead, pay attention to how you *feel* when you participate in these activities and use that as motivation to continue inviting them into your day-to-day routine for a few minutes at a time. As you move forward, select another two from the list and add those into your routine. Again, notice how you feel before, during, and after the activity.

Disclaimer: If you find yourself saying, "But I just don't have time for all of these things!" I will stop you there. You have the time, yet you choose not to prioritize your time to let joy in. Why is that? Can you commit to five to ten minutes per day of joyful activities? (Yes, just five to ten minutes is plenty as you develop self-care as a healthy habit.) We often get in our own way because of something called "conditioning." Let's explore conditioning versus character.

Conditioning vs. Character

How many times have you heard someone say, "sport builds character?" While sports often provide a container for learning qualities such as leadership, work ethic, time management, and effective communication, being an athlete does not build character.

Here's why: character is something that is within you—a defining quality or individual feature. It's what distinguishes you from another person. While other people may share similar qualities, how it manifests itself within you is, in fact, unique to you! Character, in my opinion, is the outward expression of your true Self.

If sports don't build character, what do they teach us? As noted above, sport can teach you many positive skills that you will use throughout your life. On the other hand, sport, which is its own culture or society when you stop to think about it, may lead to what is called "conditioning."

"Conditioning" is a sense of teaching or making one accustomed to certain habits or responses. Conditioning is what those outside of you teach you, rather than what you know to be true within yourself. It is the layers of lessons, expectations, pressures, and fears put on us from the time we are born.

A "condition" is also something that limits your thinking or behavior. Don't get me wrong, you have been conditioned by more than your sport, but, for this book, we will focus on examples of sport-specific conditioning and how to recognize the lessons that no longer serve you. Let's dive in.

Examples of Sport Culture Conditioning

It's important to note that the way *you* experience the world more than likely differs from how *I* experience the world. For this section, take the examples that resonate with you most and use the space below to add additional conditioned beliefs that you have been taught through sport by your coaches, teammates, or family members.

- If you aren't doing the most, you aren't doing enough.
- If you aren't performing at your best, what's the point?
- Winning is everything.
- Never stop competing! Race the person next to you. Beat them! Do you measure up to the competition?
- Sport is inherently good, inevitably leading to individual and community development.
- Push through the pain. No pain, no gain.
- Be tough! Rub some dirt on it! Don't stop!
- There's no time for rest. You'll get left behind if you choose to rest.
- Don't be so emotional – there's no place for emotions in sports.
- Make sure you're cheering for your teammates! If you aren't cheering and being loud, you aren't a good teammate.
- Be loud, communicate, and take the lead!
- Just let it go, move on, or get over it.
- Just do it! Stop thinking so much.

I could go on and on, but I'd prefer you pause to think about specific conditioned beliefs you were taught in sport. We will discuss ways to reframe these beliefs shortly. For now, simply notice your conditioning without judgment of those you learned from and of yourself for holding onto your conditioned beliefs.

What conditioned beliefs have you picked up from your sport, coach, teammates, and sport culture as a whole?

_____

_____

_____

_____

_____

_____

_____

_____

_____

_____

CHAPTER 4:

"WHY SO SENSITIVE?"

The Road Less Traveled: HSPs in Sports

When you envision the stereotypical athlete, what do you see? While this may differ from sport to sport, you may imagine this person is a great communicator, able to perform in high-pressure situations while surrounded by cheering fans, bright lights, and the expectation of winning.

Except for the celebratory win, this person is likely to be hyper-focused and is rarely rattled or showing emotion. This person has thick skin and takes criticism without so much as blinking—the tough, go-getter who isn't afraid to call out their teammate to move the team towards their goals. Overtly, this individual is outgoing and a team player. They are bold and, sometimes, in-your-face. This type of athlete is highly valued in the world of sports.

As you may have realized by now, not all athletes are made equal. What about the athlete who is naturally inclined to be on the quiet side or may experience deeper emotions than the previously described athlete? This type of athlete may find themselves overstimulated by the bright lights, loud fans, or the corrections of their coaches and teammates. They are the ones who feel the deepest joy as well as the most painful disappointment.

They not only will feel their own pain, but the pain of others as if it is their own. Typically, parents, teachers, or coaches do not teach how to navigate this type of emotion, leaving the highly sensitive athlete to fend for themself. Often, this leads to pushing their feelings down to fit the stereotype and be accepted in their sport.

This example leads me to the question: Is there no place for the highly sensitive athlete in sport? I dare say there *is* room, but the athletic community must work to change the paradigm and allow for these individuals to step into the magic of their true Selves with confidence!

As a highly sensitive athlete, I felt like I was losing an uphill battle most of the time. For example, I was told that if I wasn't on the side of the pool cheering for my teammates throughout the meet, I was a bad teammate. However, in my mind, being a *good* teammate was preparing for my race, so I could swim my heart out and score points for the team. As you can see, my approach was internal, while the beliefs of those in my environment were mainly external.

I was made to feel that expressing my emotions was detrimental to the team—that being myself wasn't good enough. I can understand that our emotions are easily picked up by others. Being a sensitive person myself, I genuinely *feel* the emotions of others. That being said, I was never advised on what to do with my feelings besides "let it go," "get over it," or "just move on to the next one."

None of those suggestions taught me to hold space for the emotion itself—instead, I learned to push it down and put on a happy face for the betterment of the group. By my junior year, I realized I would continue to experience emotions after my races (good *and* not so good emotions), so the locker room stall became a haven to let out a good cry or have some self-talk. After a few minutes, I made my way back to the pool deck and my team.

The idea that it's beneficial to your performance to repress your feelings or that it's "simple" to let it go is pervasive across sport culture. I've encountered this suggestion many times in my work as a mental performance coach. On the surface, it may seem to benefit the athlete to repress their feelings, but, beneath the surface, the emotion is building. What happens when pressure builds, one emotion pushed down on top of the other over many years?

Boom! Your emotions will find a way to escape. As humans, we're not meant to *hold* emotion for long. I will discuss this in more detail later in this book (see Chapter 5: "Sensitivity is a Superpower (in Sport & Beyond)" and Chapter 8: "Sensitive After Sport"), where I will teach you **how best** to navigate emotions in and out of sport. For now, it's essential to explore the perceptions of sensitivity in sport so we can flip the script on what it means to be a highly sensitive athlete.

TIME TO REFLECT: Use the space below to label the emotions you have felt while participating in your sport. Hindsight is 20/20. If you can remember, what did you do with or about this emotion?

For example, you may remember experiencing frustration during many matches, which led you to throw your racquet. Similarly, you may have lost a race or missed a cut time by only hundredths of a second—you found yourself experiencing anger, frustration, and disappointment, which led you to throw your goggles at the wall. Finally, conjure up a time things went well—when you felt pure joy and excitement! What was your response to this emotional experience?

SITUATION	EMOTION FELT	REACTION

Perception of Sensitivity in Sport

In today's society—particularly in the U.S.—extroversion is favored all the way from the classroom to the field to a meeting room. Susan Cain highlights this in her book, *Quiet: The Power of Introverts in a World That Can't Stop Talking*. In school, for example, you are placed in a room full of other students and bright lights with the potential for pressure around performance.

Introvert and HSP here—being called to the board to answer a math problem was my worst nightmare realized. In a meeting room, those who speak up and share their ideas with confidence are celebrated. Often, a more introverted or HSP individual will struggle to get a word in. Although, when these individuals choose to speak, listen up, as it is likely to be extra meaningful.

The same can be said for the world of sport. Sports are geared around high energy and stimulation from practice to competition. There is very little opportunity for alone time or one-on-one time with a coach, which would be beneficial to an introverted or highly sensitive athlete.

In all three scenarios, the introvert learns or is conditioned to present as extroverted or outgoing. An example of this is when introverted children are told or, rather, overhear their teacher, family, or parents of other children commenting on their "shyness." Then, these same children are encouraged to join a group to "get them out of their shell." These comments inadvertently teach the child that their natural preferences are less valid than their extroverted counterparts. This belief is affirmed by pushing a child to join a sport team and throughout the sports experience.

It's important to recognize that not all sensitive people are introverted, yet many introverts happen to be highly sensitive. You may be a highly sensitive person who is extremely outgoing when around the *right* people or in a supportive environment and gain energy from social situations. These observations, yet again, highlight individual differences—you are uniquely you!

I wanted to understand what it means to be sensitive in sport, so I conducted an informal poll of current and former athletes who resonate with being sensitive. 85% of respondents said their sensitivity was perceived as a weakness by their coach, team, or sport's culture in general. 75% of people who took the poll said they'd been told they're "too sensitive."

A similar number of individuals also stated they view their sensitive trait negatively and don't know how to use it to their advantage. *This* is why I'm writing this book—to flip the script! I want you to feel empowered by your sensitivity rather than defeated and burned out.

Based on your experience, how was sensitivity perceived in your sport or on your team? (Circle your answer)

Strength   Weakness

Have you ever been told you are "too sensitive" or to "stop being so sensitive/emotional?"

Yes   No

Do you currently know how to use your sensitive trait(s) to your advantage in sport or life?

Yes   No

The first step towards using your sensitivity to your advantage is understanding how, as a highly sensitive athlete, you have been conditioned to cover up your true Self, otherwise known as "masking."

Conditioning of Highly Sensitive Athletes

We happen to live in a world that values assimilation (e.g., asking those outside the culture or norm to change to fit into the collective) over individuality. A majority of research on masking is associated with Autism Spectrum Disorder, yet it can be applied to those with high sensitivity as well. Research suggests that, when a highly sensitive person chooses to camouflage their traits, they may experience depression, anxiety, burnout, and exhaustion.

Masking requires concentration and self-control, which can be mentally and physically draining. Masking occurs in sport when an individual covers up or pushes down their true Self to be embraced within their team's culture by their coach, team, or fans. Masking may also occur when an athlete experiences a mental health issue such as depression, anxiety, an eating disorder, or other mental illness (i.e., bipolar disorder, self-harm, etc.). They cover up their true experience or feelings with a smile or sense of humor.

Let's use another memory to better describe masking in the real world. I have always been extremely sensitive to rejection (something I've learned may be a symptom of ADHD—known as Rejection Sensitivity Dysphoria). It all started back in elementary school when I would crawl into a little ball if a friend said "no" to a playdate. I had barely enough courage to pick up the phone to call them, so when they said they couldn't (no matter the reason), I just about lost it.

A spiral of shame would set in. Thoughts like, "she must not like me," "I'm not good enough for her," and more filled my mind. I also had an extremely tough time getting in trouble or being yelled at by an authority figure. I did everything in my power to avoid this, yet it would happen on occasion.

Why is this relevant? Because I will never forget the times my swim coach yelled at me. I couldn't handle the shame and embarrassment. I wanted to disappear. But practice must go on, so what did I do? I put on my goggles and cried, letting them fill with tears.

I'm giving myself a big hug now as I write this because my younger Self really needed it at the time. I wanted someone to tell me it was okay to cry and that I could feel my feelings and let them go. Instead, my tears filled my goggles as I pushed off the wall. No one could know my secret; my goggles were my mask.

Highly sensitive individuals tend to experience low self-esteem when not valued in the culture as their sensitivity is made to feel abnormal. As mentioned above, being highly sensitive or introverted is less valued in sport than the extroverted, social, less emotional, team player personality.

When you choose to be a member of a team, you are signing up for an experience that involves being surrounded by others in a highly structured, competitive, and stimulating environment. However, does that mean there is no room for an introvert or highly sensitive person to be themselves? I don't think so. Sports bring people of all backgrounds together in the face of a common goal. I believe there is space for **all** personality types to thrive in sports. It's time to flip the script on the conditioned belief that those who are extroverted or less sensitive are the most successful in sport and life outside of sport.

Challenges of Being a Highly Sensitive Athlete

A highly sensitive athlete puts on a mask when they feel their sensitive nature isn't valued or accepted. They do so to protect themselves, yet masking may inadvertently lead to more harm than good because you cannot be yourself, depleting your energy and knocking you out of alignment with your authentic Self and soul's purpose.

I've listed the most common challenges of the highly sensitive athlete in the sports world and have left a few lines blank to add additional challenges you have faced personally.

- You are being dismissed concerning injuries, illness, or exhaustion. You can perceive things in your body others can't.
- You are easily overstimulated.
- You may need more sleep on average.
- You have deep empathy for others and experience guilt and shame for needing to take care of your Self.
- You carry a lack of self-trust.
- You have blurry boundaries. For example, you say "yes" often when your gut is telling you "no!" You choose to overextend yourself (socially or otherwise) when it's clear you need time to be alone and recharge.
- You hold your Self to higher standards and feel shame/embarrassment around mistakes.
- _____
- _____

To connect these challenges to the conditioning of sports culture, I want to provide a deeper explanation for two—the first being "being dismissed regarding injury or illness." Have you ever been injured and unable to compete in your sport? Consider your experience. How were you treated by teammates, coaches, or even by yourself?

This challenge is especially relevant to less apparent injuries, such as a shoulder injury that doesn't require surgery or a mental health issue such as depression and anxiety. A common belief in sport is "do what it takes to get back on the field/in the pool/on the court" or "push through the pain."

If, on the outside, everything seems okay, people may dismiss your injury and put pressure on you to get back in the game. As a highly sensitive athlete, you may feel your pain on a deeper level or be quicker to notice something doesn't feel right, even if everyone is telling you, "You're ready." Only **you** know when you're truly ready, yet this stands in contrast to the conditioning mentioned earlier.

Recognizing the importance of learning the difference within yourself between fatigue and pain and having honest accountability at the moment is important. This isn't about "getting out of practice" or "sitting out a set" just for the heck of it.

If you feel compelled to use an injury to do this, I invite you to reflect on "why." What is this behavior telling you? In the next section, you will learn how to set and hold boundaries, stand in your power, have confident conversations, and recognize what is or is not suitable for you.

The second challenge I'd like to explore is the lack of self-trust. As mentioned in Chapter 2, highly sensitive children are often conditioned to believe their sensitivity is a burden—that they are less valued than those who are less sensitive. A child may be told he or she is "too sensitive," or to "suck it up," and then be forced to interact with other children in a way that doesn't align with their true Self (i.e., put into groups or on a team upon being labeled "shy" or "not social enough"). As a result, the child can resort to putting on their mask and disconnect from their sensitive traits.

Ever met someone who said, "I haven't cried in years?" While there are plenty of reasons for this, often it's because they've put up a wall, blocking out their ability to feel or understand deeply to fit into a culture where being less emotional or more outgoing is appreciated.

Once an HSP puts on their mask, they begin to lose trust in their body's signals of pain, (emotional) discomfort, or exhaustion. When you're unable to tune into the wisdom of your body, you are less able to recognize that which you truly need. As a result, a highly sensitive athlete may experience physical illness, depression, anxiety, or substance abuse in their lifetime.

The pervading theme of the above challenges is the lack of trust or inability to tune into your body's signals to rest, say "no," or the need to feel your emotions (i.e., *cry*). So, how can you overcome these barriers in sport and life outside of sport? Go inward and uncover your innate power and wisdom!

Author's note: *I feel I can't gloss over the idea of masking without mentioning the time we are living in, currently. The use of literal masks throughout the COVID-19 pandemic has brought up a deep exploration of the word "masking." We use a mask to protect ourselves and others. For many, it's a bother, while, for others, it provides a great deal of safety. Now, imagine the figurative mask worn by highly sensitive athletes—the mask makes them feel safe in an environment that would typically be overwhelming and even violating.*

I've seen memes and TikToks exemplifying this with introverts and HSPs jumping for joy at the idea of wearing a mask to the grocery store so they can avoid social interaction with ease. While I laughed at these videos, they also represent feelings of the collective—that society's expectations of people require you to interact, be social and polite by sharing small talk and a smile. Wearing a mask has provided HSPs and introverts with comfort like no other—a mask has allowed HSPs to be their true Self and limit social over-stimulation.

*On the other hand, figurative masking in sport is **preventing** this and is an act of **hiding** and even taking on traits of extroversion/outgoingness to blend into the crowd. For the purpose of this book, we will focus on removing the **figurative** mask so you can step into your true Self with confidence in and out of sport!*

CHAPTER 5:

SENSITIVITY IS A SUPERPOWER (IN SPORT AND BEYOND)

I f you've made it this far, it's clear you resonate with the sensitive trait in some way, whether you are highly sensitive or you are the coach or parent to a sensitive athlete. You've gained awareness around what it means to be sensitive and learned how the culture and attitudes surrounding a sensitive athlete play a role in their mental and emotional health.

Now, it's time to *reframe* this perception of sensitivity as a "burden" and step into the **power** of your sensitive Self. Your **magic** lies beneath the mask. Are you ready to claim your magic and let your light shine? If so, follow me on the path as I help you unmask and shine bright for the world to see.

The Truth About Confidence

In my work with college athletes, the number one block to performance is confidence or lack thereof. The athletes who reach out to me report struggling with confidence. "It fluctuates," they often say. "If I'm playing well, I feel confident. But if I'm not playing well, I feel terrible."

Based on my studies in the fields of psychology and sport psychology over the last decade, in addition to my 14 years as an athlete, I've learned an important lesson: confidence isn't dependent on performance. Or, at least, it isn't designed to be.

Let's revisit the conditioning of sports culture where there is a focus on winning, doing your best, and beating your opponent. What happens when you don't do your best? It may not always be overt, but often, there is less cheering and more sympathy. You don't have people coming up to you and telling you, "Great job!" You experience more of the conversations around what you can do better next time.

While this is helpful regarding your growth as an athlete, it inadvertently teaches you that winning, or a personal best, leads to **feeling** your best or most confident. It's when you feel most appreciated by those around you and, similarly, within yourself.

It's time to dismantle the belief that confidence comes from **outside** yourself or is based on your performance. Confidence lives *within* you. Confidence is the **fire** that drives you and ignites your soul and the powerhouse that moves you forward each day. Simply, **you** are enough, and you have all you need within you. When you build trust within yourself and tune into your body's innate wisdom, you will recognize that some things are outside your control (like winning).

In its simplest form, confidence is your belief in your Self. By believing in your Self, you can move through obstacles to reach your goals (also known as mental toughness). Confidence gives you the strength to let go of mistakes and move forward towards your aspirations. I believe that we all can access confidence, no matter our circumstances, because confidence is a choice.

Choose to look inward and acknowledge who **you** are and where your **power** lies. You can make this choice much easier by releasing the conditioning that limits your strength or asks you to rely on your performance or the opinions of others.

Can you take a good look in the mirror and choose to love yourself? Can you choose to see the magic that lies within? By shedding the weight of all that no longer serves you, you will find it much easier to access and claim your confidence.

Tools to Claim Your Confidence

The above is often easier said than done, but only if you don't have the tools to let go of the conditioning holding you back. Here are my top tools for claiming your confidence.

- Change the way you talk to yourself from "I can't do this" to "I trust my training and know I can push through!"

- Power pose! We can feel confident in the mind *and* body, so powerful body language is essential.
- Be your own #1 fan. Start your day with a motivating mirror message (e.g., "I am empowered. I am strong. I am great at what I do. I am going to make the most out of this day.")
- Start a Confidence Jar. At the end of each day, write one thing you are proud of yourself for accomplishing and put it in the jar. Revisit the contents of the jar as needed (e.g., before practice in the middle of the season when things are super tough or before heading off to your championships).
- Rebuild trust with yourself. You can start this by keeping promises to yourself. Start small. Congratulate yourself for keeping the promise. Feel into a space of gratitude and compassion.

A Sensitive Person's Superpowers

Now that you know it's within everyone's destiny to feel empowered by claiming your confidence, let's acknowledge the specific superpowers of the highly sensitive athlete.

- Empathic and intuitive (when accessed)
- Understanding
- Good listener
- High awareness (internal and external)
- Team player
- Able to anticipate an opponent or teammate's next move
- Spotting and fixing mistakes
- High productivity
- "Coachable"/ Follows rules

These are all potential strengths of highly sensitive athletes who have stepped into their confidence and released conditioning holding them back from being their most true and powerful Selves. In sport, you may have learned to focus on areas needing improvement, and for a good reason. Without this awareness, how would you make the necessary adjustments to grow?

However, do you want to know a secret to success? You need to direct your attention towards your **strengths** (aka your **superpowers**)! When you feed your superpowers with the focus and energy they deserve, they only get more **powerful**. This will give you the momentum you need to **level up** in all areas of your life.

List all the ways your sensitivity has **enhanced** your athletic performance, school/work, and day-to-day life. Nothing is too small. Go deep! What have you *noticed* more of, *felt* more of, or *understood* more of?

_____

_____

_____

_____

_____

_____

_____

_____

_____

_____

The Empowered Highly Sensitive Athlete

It's your time to shine, highly sensitive athlete! **Disclaimer:** Let go of your need and want to **change** your coaches, teammates, or sport culture in general. This may or may not happen while you are competing. The beliefs and behaviors of others are never within your control. Who or what *can* you control? You, and only you.

You have the ability to look within and choose confidence each day. You have the power to let go of the beliefs that no longer serve you and focus on your **strengths** that will move you forward in sport and life. This is what it's like living an empowered life rather than giving away your power to your performance or the people around you.

To finish up this chapter, let's hone in on *how* to use the superpowers of the highly sensitive trait to your advantage in sport.

- Empathic and intuitive (when accessed): Being in tune with the feelings of others around you allows you to provide an ear or a shoulder for a teammate in need. You may intuitively pick up on the change in energy throughout practice or a game.

When you notice this change, choose to influence the energy in the best interest of yourself and your team. How can you do this? Communication and body language!

- High awareness (internal and external): I can't stress the importance of awareness enough in and out of sport. Awareness of your strengths and weaknesses is a must. Awareness of your emotions **in the present moment** is extremely valuable, as it allows you to choose how to respond (to said emotion) appropriately.

Awareness of your opponents on the court, field, or mat is equally important so you can select your next "move." Awareness of your teammates will allow you to play more cohesively and connect on and off the "field."

Want to build your awareness? Begin a daily meditation practice or try breathwork! Daily journaling to understand your emotions and behaviors better is also a helpful strategy.

- Team player: A highly sensitive athlete understands deeply, listens deeply, and cares deeply. This can lead to being an effective team member if their sensitive trait isn't devalued. Whether they are in a leadership position or not, you can rely on a highly sensitive athlete to be there off and on the "field."
- Anticipating: This is useful for sports like basketball, soccer, squash, tennis, and wrestling. Anticipating the moves of your opponent will give you the

upper hand. **Tune in** to this trait in the moment and watch your performance soar!

- Spotting and fixing mistakes: This speaks for itself. If you cannot recognize a mistake or a skill that requires adjustment, you won't improve in this area. Your keen observation skills are extremely valuable in sport. Use them to your advantage!
- Coachable: I always considered myself to be coachable. I followed the rules, listened, and grasped the concept of each practice set quickly. Doing this allowed me to be effective (or productive) right away and make the most of practice.

If you play a team sport, you can use this ability to enhance your teammates' effectiveness. Give them insight or help them understand by asking or answering questions. You don't always need to rely on your coach for the answers. Become accountable for yourself and guide others to do the same.

Overall, I intend to help you reframe any negative perceptions of being highly sensitive. Your sensitivity is a **superpower** if you choose to claim it. Like any classic superhero, they first had to accept their powers for what they were before they could use them for good. **Claim it** and sink into the energy of your superpower every day.

In an attempt to remain aligned with your strengths, you will also need to consider the types of situations that have the potential to stifle your abilities. Think Superman versus Kryptonite.

Take me, for example. My sensitive superpower is **connection**. Authentically communicating with and supporting people is my gift, and it brings me immense energy and enthusiasm. However, I am naturally introverted, and I absorb the energy and emotions of others quite easily (if I'm not careful).

This insight has led me to set boundaries in terms of the quantity (and quality, for that matter) of people I connect and communicate with to avoid overloading my system and depleting my mental, physical, and emotional energy. Over time, I learned that I need to recharge my battery in the absence of people while replenishing my energy by relaxing with my dog, Calvin, nighttime baths, dancing in my living room, and daily outdoor walks.

Your turn! Considering your superpower(s) and other personal characteristics, what is your kryptonite? How does it affect you?

_____

_____

_____

_____

_____

_____

_____

_____

If it is not possible to avoid, what can you do to offset the effects of your kryptonite?

_____

_____

_____

_____

_____

_____

_____

CHAPTER 6:

A MESSAGE TO COACHES

This is a note to coaches who have highly sensitive athletes on your team. Hint: If you're a coach, I will bet you have at least one! Remember, 15% to 20% of people have the highly sensitive trait. If you don't easily view anyone as highly sensitive, they may be masking to fit into their team's culture or that of the sport as a whole.

You may also apply this to your home life if your child appears to be highly sensitive; whether they are an athlete or not, the following advice will positively impact your child and the relationship you have with them.

This is an invitation for you to look within yourself and help change the narrative. As a coach, you hold stock in the conditioning of your athletes. You are a teacher and guide. You also have authority. Whatever you teach them, they will soak up.

If you teach them to cover up their sensitivity, they will. If you provide a supportive and accepting space for their sensitivity to *shine*, they will **let it shine**. When they are allowed to step into their authentic Self, watch them grow with immense speed. The greatest gift you can give your highly sensitive athlete is to allow them to step into their true power and potential by valuing their sensitivity.

If you intend to bring out the best in *all* your athletes, you must acknowledge and *celebrate* their differences. Notice how they are different from one another and how they are, more importantly, different from you. Different does not equal bad and is not something to be fearful of.

Our differences invite us to open up and explore the intricacies of culture, people, and the Universe as a whole. While it may require more effort, the rewards will be bountiful for your team and for the athlete you have invited into your team. If you have the best interest of your athletes at heart and truly do what you do "for the athletes," keep this in your mind and heart as you move forward in your career and life.

Greater awareness of what it means to empower introverted and highly sensitive athletes in sports is necessary. As coaches and administrators, even family members, you can learn to recognize and validate the experience of a highly sensitive athlete, which will allow them to remove the mask and step up to the plate in all their greatness. Isn't that what you want from your athletes?

As a mental performance coach, I sit across the room (or on the other end of the computer screen) from hundreds of athletes. Not one session or person has been the same as another. There are no carbon copies when it comes to human beings.

Recognizing individual differences keeps me on my toes and makes my job exciting! While I may share similar skills for the athlete to implement, their experience and journey henceforth (upon learning the skill) will be unique. Rather than telling them what to do, I must first sit and listen.

I hear their story. I *see* them for who they truly are. I never attempt to change them. They are perfect as is. They do not need to be fixed because they *aren't* broken. They are enough and always will be.

Once I've heard them out, we will go back and forth a bit, but I'm always responding to the information they've given me rather than basing my next move on what I'm *hoping* they will do, say, or be. I need to leave expectations and preconceived notions at the door.

Human beings are complicated in all the best ways. As a coach, it's your job to hold space for your athletes *as they are* and provide guidance and support that will **enhance** their life and athletic experience. It is *not* your job to change *who* they are to fit your vision.

Reminder: A highly sensitive athlete will show up and do **amazing things** if they are valued for who they are. If they are made to feel ashamed of their sensitivity or like they need to change to "fit in" or "be a better athlete," this may lead to serious mental health consequences. Let your athletes, the people you invited to be a member of your team, be themselves while, at the same time, providing guidance and support regarding the physical skills and performance of your sport.

If you find that your athlete's highly sensitive traits hold them back from stepping into a particular role (e.g., captain), have an open and honest conversation. When given a chance and considering they are **ready** to do so, many highly sensitive people will learn how to lean into that role.

On the other hand, it may not be something the person wants or feels comfortable doing. For example, being an open/loud communicator just wasn't in my repertoire back in high school or college, and I was, unsurprisingly, never voted as a captain—I was more than okay with this, clearly. Show your athlete respect and consideration through an authentic, one on one conversation rather than making them feel like they "did something wrong" or "are no good," which they may believe if left to their own imagination rather than receiving clear answers from you.

Overall, it is a choice to cultivate an environment that supports and values the individual differences of your athletes. How can you support your highly sensitive athletes to help them show up as their authentic selves, allowing them to reach their full potential in sport and life?

Action steps you can take:

- Listen with empathy (open ears and an open heart).
- Ask open-ended questions about how they feel.
- Make it a priority to get to know your athletes on an individual level. Yes, this can take time and effort, especially depending on the size of your team, but it's **worth it**!

List any ideas that come to your mind:

- _____
- _____
- _____

CHAPTER 7:

THE ROAD AHEAD

The time has come. It's time for you to move on from a sport for which you devoted more than a decade of your life. For some athletes, this may bring long-awaited relief from the 5:30 am wakeup calls to jump in a cold pool (for all my swimmers out there), the intense daily grind, or from the sport itself.

On the other hand, some athletes may face a deep sense of loss and a lack of direction or motivation after leaving their sport behind. These feelings may pop up for you whether you fulfilled your eligibility, were cut from a team, or experienced a career-ending injury. Regardless, it is time to say goodbye and, deep down, you aren't prepared. If this is you, know you are not alone.

While I was relieved to no longer smell like chlorine, jump in a cold pool before the sun came up, or walk outside with wet hair in two-degree weather, I was also met with a deeply painful sense of grief for what I had lost. I lost my first love, my safe space, my protector. I lost my second home.

At the time, it was hard to verbalize how I felt. After touching the wall of my last race, emotion overcame me. I could barely stop crying for the next 12 hours. We had one more day of competition, though, so I pushed away my tears because it felt like no one understood, not even my coaches. People must've thought I was crying because I hadn't swum my best.

While it was upsetting to end on a less-than-high note, it wasn't the complete picture. The tears were flowing because of what I had lost. None of my teammates had finished competing yet, so I felt alone in this. That is until one of my teammates swam her final 1650 (the mile). I remember she walked up to me and said, "I'm sorry. I didn't understand until now." And we cried together.

The student-athlete experience is unique. I often find that people on the outside have difficulty understanding what an athlete may go through unless they have experienced it. Dear former athletes: I see you. Letting go and moving on from your sport is rarely easy, especially if you've identified as an athlete most of your life.

Sport Transition in the Age of COVID-19

As I write this book, it's the beginning of 2021. We've been in quarantine due to COVID-19 for nearly a year. Working in college athletics, I have a front-row seat to the chaos that is college sports this year. Spring 2020 seniors or fifth-year student-athletes had what they believed would be their final season ripped out from underneath them.

While the NCAA has since reinstated a year of eligibility, I know many athletes made the hard decision to walk away to pursue other ventures (aka start living their lives). Some were unable to make another year of school and sport work due to financial or other reasons. If this was your experience, I must say I am truly sorry this happened. I'm sorry you didn't get the opportunity to play your final season in the way you had always imagined.

At the beginning of quarantine, I encountered coaches telling their athletes to "get perspective; people are dying," only days after they had lost their sport. At that point, I was *this close* (insert image of my pointer finger and thumb less than a millimeter away from each other) to losing my *shiz*. I write this in no way to diminish the severity of the collective's circumstances. Rather, it was disheartening to see coaches, who were highly respected by their athletes, invalidating or brushing off the loss of their athletes.

A piece of them *had* died the moment they were told their final season was over and, for some, before it had even really started. There would be no fanfare, no medals, no applause, as circumstances did not allow them to reach their senior season goals. What makes it even sadder is that so many people failed to notice.

To those of you who lost your senior or final season in 2020 (or 2021, as many sports and schools aren't competing this year, either), hear this: I see you. Your feelings are valid. Drop the mask, and allow yourself to feel your feelings just as they are. Ask for support and learn how to move forward. The only way out is *through*.

The remainder of this chapter and "Chapter 8: Sensitive After Sport" will provide you with the knowledge and resources to make a positive transition into life **after** sport.

Making the Best of Your Transition

I spent three years of my doctoral studies researching the transition out of sport. It was a cathartic experience as I had yet to shed the emotional weight of *my* transition out of swimming. I often say my purpose was to become the person I needed back then, and I'd like to think I have done just that.

Through my research and work with collegiate athletes over the last five years, I can now share the resources I wish I had when I finished swimming eight years ago. The following few sections come directly from my research, including my doctoral dissertation. I conducted "think tank" groups with former athletes about their perceptions of their transition out of collegiate sport. The results provide insight into the resources and knowledge that college athletes felt would enhance the transition process.

Awareness of Shift in Identity

Concerning the transition out of sport, the end may be in sight, or an athlete may experience a traumatic and unexpected end to their career. Either way, there are limited resources for athletes to plan for life after sport, and, more often than not, an athlete won't want to think about the end of their athletic career until it is, well, over. Therefore, they are less likely to learn or use coping strategies to positively navigate their transition to life after sport.

Additionally, research demonstrates that the impact of significant life events may linger over two years following the experience. Increased awareness, specifically self-awareness of one's thoughts, feelings, strengths, and weaknesses have shown to benefit individuals encountering negative life events. These individuals tend to use coping skills and resources sooner and more efficiently than individuals with poor emotional self-awareness. They are also more aware of the stressful events before or while they were experienced, leading them to employ coping skills before facing the full impact of the event.

The day-to-day schedule of an athlete typically looks like this: wake up, train, eat, school, eat, train again, eat again, school or work, and sleep. Repeat. It's structured and strategic. It's anything but **slow** and **still**.

After the final competition, you'd think it would be easy to maintain the go-go-go. The opposite is often true. Gone are the days of structured workouts with the accountability of your coach and teammates. After sport? It's up to **you**.

A term many athletes throw around is NARP—Non-Athlete Regular Person. It simply refers to anyone who isn't a competitive athlete. When an athlete hangs up their "goggles," does that mean they become a NARP?

You'll find differing opinions across the former athlete community.

For some, being a NARP comes as a relief after more than a decade of early mornings, high-intensity training sessions, and strict schedules. For others, the idea of letting go of their identity as an athlete brings up feelings of anxiety and even fear. Some may ask, "Who am I without my sport?"

Whether the individual agrees or not, in one way or another, they have become a NARP—someone who has (a bit) more control over their schedule, choosing to exercise at their leisure rather than being required to jump in the pool at precisely 5:30 am.

Because of this, many former athletes may find it challenging to stay physically active in life after sport. We must support these individuals in their attempt to maintain overall health and well-being after the final buzzer.

Circling back to chapter one on athletic identity, student-athletes with a strong and exclusive athlete identity may experience long-term effects following sport transition. Feelings experienced may include a sense of failure (if goals are not met), depression, and isolation. Following the transition, athletes reported moving from the role of an athlete to a "normal student," or NARP, but this change in role was not easy for many athletes.

The more they identified with the role of athlete, the more challenging they found the exit from the sport. Reframing your identity can only be done, however, if an individual is *aware* of the change and responds to this adjustment, making self-awareness and planning for change all that more important.

Activity: Getting to Know You

You have dedicated years of your time, energy, and attention to your sport. You push(ed) your body and mind to the limit day in and day out, overriding your body's signals to rest to reach your performance goals. As an athlete, you've been taught to direct your energy and attention into the **big wins**—get the best time, win the race, beat your opponent! This mindset conditioned you to overlook the beauty of life around you—the beauty within **you**.

I invite you to spend some time thinking about yourself. Who are you? What makes you *you*? What brings you **joy**? Make a list.

This list may differ from what you value concerning your sport, and that's okay. Challenge yourself to open your eyes **wide** and broaden your view to get a clear picture of who you are or who you want to be now.

Who are you? *What* makes you *you*?

Put on some music (I recommend Chillhop on Youtube). Set a 15-minute timer. Connect with your true, authentic Self. Take a **deep dive** inward!

_____

_____

_____

_____

_____

_____

_____

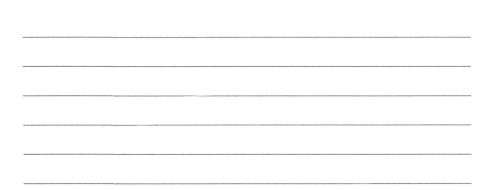

Rethinking Exercise/Movement

The second (sub)theme of my dissertation research involved reframing what you perceive to be exercise. Athletes become accustomed to a certain type and intensity level of workouts that help them progress towards performance goals, so, upon transitioning out of sport, it's important to acknowledge a potential shift in motivation, purpose, and like or dislike for particular exercise activities.

It's also possible that you will experience inconsistent thoughts, beliefs, or attitudes regarding "real" exercise. For example, you may struggle to view light and moderate movements, such as walking or yoga, as a form of exercise that will benefit you as much as your sport training did. Finding a way to bridge the gap of understanding of how "different" forms of physical activity will benefit you in post-collegiate sport life could lead to increased enjoyment, allowing you to stick with physical activity over time.

Well-known for her research on shame and vulnerability, Brene Brown defines shame as "the intensely painful feeling or experience of believing we are flawed and therefore unworthy of connection and belonging." Don't be alarmed if, due to your conditioning of being mentally and physically tough, an attachment to this ideal outside of sports could lead to feelings of shame or guilt because you are no longer participating in similarly intense forms of exercise.

Brown highlights awareness of these social expectations and feelings towards such norms as paramount to developing shame resilience. For now, simply notice these feelings, write about them, or get up and move your body (dance, shake, walk) to move the energy out!

Re-defining exercise was a major challenge for me, personally. For two years, I lived in a city, walking upwards of six miles per day to and from school, before, all of a sudden, I had an "aha" moment! I would arrive home exhausted and could never make myself get up and exercise. Then, it finally hit me that *walking* was exercise!

Three years later, walking outside has become my go-to form of movement. I let go of my old ways of thinking and realized that red in the face, heavy breathing on the cold floor was **not** the only way to exercise (nor was it necessarily the best option for me). Changing my beliefs around exercise released me from the hold of shame and guilt I felt for choosing to move in a way that my body was calling for!

Activity: Spend 15 minutes outside—no music, no dog, no teammate or family. No distractions.

> Slow down your pace.
> Look around.
> What do you see?
> What do you hear?
> What do you smell?
> How do you feel?

Following your walk, scan the QR code for a short, guided audio process to help you tune into your body!

Your turn! What is *your* definition of movement in the absence of sport? How does your body *want* to move?

Building Community After Sport

Next, the athletes who participated in my research highlighted the importance of building community and authentic connection to alleviate feelings of isolation or loneliness after losing their team environment. From the moment you joined a team, you became a part of the athletic/sports community; this feeling of support, based on sharing common goals and values, is (typically) consistent throughout your athletic career.

On the other hand, when you transition out of sport, this support system is no longer a given aspect of your life unless you make the active choice to find or maintain that community. This sense of community plays a role in an individual's motivation to exercise because former athletes aren't typically used to training alone (particularly at the college level—professional athletes in individual sports may, in fact, train alone).

Athletes who participated in my study stated they wanted to either remain connected or to once again feel connected to a community that they had lost upon graduating from college and leaving their team behind. While some may argue that you have the potential to remain friends with individuals from your team, it's also clear that maintaining friendships when not living near one another, such as in the same dorm, apartment, or a quick walk down the block, presents a challenge. When individuals begin their careers and adjust to a new schedule, remaining connected is even more difficult for many in a 9-5 job.

In the "real world," friendships or connections are not instantaneous and take time and effort to develop. In some workplaces, such as those that are fast-paced and high pressure, friendships may never form as people tend to focus on the work presented to them.

As shocking and confusing as this may seem to you, at 22, I came to the realization that I didn't know how to make friends outside of school or swimming, both of which were structured to *help* me build relationships. Rather than expecting the athlete to "figure it out" (which is made even more difficult when dealing with the loss of your sport and support system in your teammates), providing space(s) for former athletes to connect and build up a community with people that share similar values and goals can be very valuable.

I invite you to check out the many "life after sport" Instagram pages, such as The Hidden Opponent, Her Sports Story, Playoff Dating App, The Virago Project, MyHuddle, and individuals who work specifically with former athletes, such as myself. We hope to bridge this gap through group programs and online platforms and bring former athletes together in community once more!

Authentic Connection & Shared Values

Every sport comes with its own culture and experiences. Nonetheless, some can argue that the overall culture of collegiate athletics lends itself to certain values such as determination, resilience, goal orientation, passion, and pride in one's program and oneself. These values tend to apply to personal and professional lives outside of sport.

Likewise, it's reasonable to assume that some of your values are developed over time spent with your teammates, coaches, and in the athletic domain. Because of this, I found that former athletes wanted to surround themselves with individuals with similar values (i.e., other former athletes, regardless of sport).

Values can also be referred to as the principles that tend to guide one's behavior. These types of values are closely related to motivation. They are typically consistent over time and situation, although there is potential for adjustment in values when an individual is faced with a new environment.

An awareness of one's values throughout the transition process can lead to an increase in well-being and physical activity levels because values are "super goals" and act as catalysts for putting goals into action. Suppose you feel that remaining physically active is within your value system. In that case, connecting with individuals with similar values may increase the chance of maintaining exercise routines by setting goals and remaining accountable within your new environment.

Awareness of Values / Goals Activity

What do you value? Pull up that playlist again and set a 15-minute timer! What matters to you? What is important to you regarding your life as a whole, your purpose in life or career, and relationships/friendships?

Detail the characteristics that are most meaningful to you. Be specific —*why* do these things matter to you?

You may notice your values aren't in line with what others taught over the years, and that's **okay** (or they might, and that's okay, too). This activity is about what *you* truly value and believe in. You can revisit this list as you move forward on your path of self-discovery!

_____

_____

_____

_____

_____

_____

_____

_____

_____

Develop Habits with Accountability

The final theme of my dissertation research involved developing and maintaining healthy habits outside of sport. Your daily life was intentionally structured as an athlete to provide a routine, potentially to turn these routines into habits. Waking up on time, getting to practice, doing the work and doing it well, and all of the steps in between become habits of mind, body, and conditioning. After losing the structure of your sport, many athletes feel lost and ask, "What do I do now?" This may be in terms of career planning, daily life, or exercise.

The assumption is that, because you exercised as a by-product of participating in sport, you know "how" to exercise and can do it in the absence of a coach. However, research asserts that athletes train day in and day out because they're provided structure from a coach, whether your head sport coach or a strength and conditioning coach (and any additional coaches/staff that provide structure). You were also used to participating in workouts alongside teammates who provided additional support and accountability.

How, then, can we assume that this behavior will translate beyond the sport realm? For some former student-athletes, the lack of structure may cause anxiety about working out or trying new forms of exercise on their own, leading to decreased levels of self-efficacy or autonomy and, in turn, declining motivation to exercise overall.

Research also indicates the value of finding a replacement for the accountability provided by your coach, team, and sports goals. Former athletes reported they felt a sense of accountability, or even obligation, to get up and be at practice on time, putting in the work as instructed and training alongside their teammates.

Participants highlighted that being surrounded by their teammates working just as hard with an overall sense of motivating energy led them to continue to train hard at each practice. Therefore, it would be helpful to identify and form groups of like-minded individuals following the loss of your team to enhance a sense of accountability to participate in other forms of exercise.

In her book, *The Four Tendencies*, Gretchen Rubin distinguishes between four tendencies for developing and maintaining habits. Particular to many athletes is the obliger tendency. Obligers can maintain a behavior when they are held accountable by someone else, such as their coach or teammates; this same behavior is challenging to uphold, however, when individuals attempt to keep themselves accountable with no external motivator. This speaks to the importance of doing something you enjoy and find easy to do each day and the use of external accountability—at the least, the buddy system.

Cultivating your support systems outside of sports is helpful as a means to hold yourself accountable. Let go of the need to "be tough" or "make it happen" yourself! Attempting to force yourself to stay motivated and be physically active in the absence of the team support you had (potentially) for over a decade is a recipe for failure. This was 100% my experience—I *needed* external support and guidance, which doesn't make me "less than" anyone else.

Although it may stand in contrast to the mentally tough attitude typically expected of athletes, asking for support shows true strength rather than braving the wilderness (of life after sport) alone.

CHAPTER 8:

SENSITIVE AFTER SPORT

The transition may be particularly difficult if you are a highly sensitive athlete, yet, in line with the theme of this book, you can prepare yourself to manage this time in your life effectively. As the saying goes, change is hard. Or is it? Over the last year, I've realized it's the **resistance** to change, not the change itself.

Despite this, change or transitions may feel **extra** hard to a highly sensitive athlete. Why? Remember what it means to be highly sensitive. You feel emotions at the deepest of levels. A highly sensitive athlete may also struggle when it comes to changing environments. You've been competing with the same people and in the same environment for years.

While you wore a mask (at times or all the time), you also grew comfortable with your surroundings and learned how to navigate challenges thrown at you. As you leave your comfort zone and enter a new environment, there is the potential for experiencing anxiety due to the overstimulation of managing new experiences, people, and places. You'll also have to decide if your new environment is a place where you can show up as your true, sensitive Self.

To play devil's advocate (with myself), you may actually **thrive** in your transition out of sport as a highly sensitive athlete. Now, you can do things at your own pace or to your liking. If you go to a gym where the lights are way too bright or they play horribly loud music, you can switch gyms or even work out at home. You have options! This aspect of the transition may go much more smoothly.

The challenge lies in the emotional weight you may carry into your life after sport. Can you let go of all that was so you can show up fully in your life **now**?

Learning to Let Go

The loss of your sport may bring up emotions you have yet to feel in your lifetime. The first step is recognizing what the end of your athletic career means to you.

If you don't feel able or prepared enough to acknowledge your emotions around this loss, I invite you to reach out for support. I advocate for working with a therapist, coach, sport psychology professional, or holistic practitioner as you navigate this transition.

I've provided space here to write down anything and everything you do feel comfortable recognizing on your own. Set a 10 to a 15-minute timer and let the words flow out onto the page. If writing doesn't come naturally to you, pick up your phone and record a voice memo. Speak your feelings into existence. What comes to the surface? There is no wrong answer as all your feelings are valid.

Beautiful job. This step is essential because you have no chance of letting them go without awareness of your thoughts and feelings. Despite what others may have taught you, emotions are meant to be honored and **felt fully**. This is the process of letting go.

Emotions = Energy in Motion

If you were to honor the emotion in the moment, it would take approximately 90 seconds for this emotion to dissipate. Sounds nice, right? Why, then, do our emotions come cascading back hours, days, months, or even years later?

Our emotions are **not meant** to be repressed. Like a volcano eruption, if you push your emotions down, again and again, adding more and more internal pressure, they will force their way to the surface whether you like it or not. As an athlete, you were taught to leave your emotions at the door or to "just forget about it."

While it may have been helpful on the court, field, or pool, you are left with stagnant energy of past experiences of anger, frustration, disappointment, sadness, and anxiety. When these emotions aren't promptly felt and allowed to *move* out of the body, the energy becomes **stuck** and slowly but surely wreaks havoc on a physical and emotional level.

Now, as you transition out of your sport, you have the opportunity to honor your feelings in the moment and let them go. "But I'm an athlete, which means I'm tough. I don't need to feel my feelings. I'm fine. I'm over it." You may *think* so, but emotions don't live in the **mind**. They are felt in the **body**.

True strength lies in recognizing how you feel, facing it head-on, and letting it go. True strength is asking for support as you navigate your emotions. As an athlete, you always had a coach who provided guidance and support along the way—after sport is no different. While awareness of your emotions and behavior patterns is important, it doesn't do much good if you don't have the tools to navigate them in the moment.

Often, we get stuck in a shame or judgment spiral, which feels defeating rather than encouraging. *This* is why finding the right mentor is a huge step in your healing. They will help you become aware of your emotions, teach you how to release them, and then show you ways to embody your true Self.

If you want to avoid the impending meltdown of pent-up emotions, it's clear you need to **release** your emotions. The question is, "how?" These are the top three techniques I teach and guide my clients through as they navigate life after sport.

Just breathe.
Move your body.
Energy healing.

Breathwork has played a pivotal role in my personal healing journey. Before March of 2020, I had never heard of it. I signed up for a workshop that was meant to be a way to connect with like-minded women in a virtual space. Who would have thought it would be the first of *many* Zoom calls (quarantine began only a few days later)?

We started the call with meditation, something I had been doing somewhat inconsistently for a year and a half, but I couldn't get the habit to stick. Then, the facilitator introduced a breathwork sequence called 4-7-8 breathing. Breathe in for four seconds, hold for seven seconds, and breathe out for eight seconds.

This was the first time I had held my breath in this way since swimming ended. My mind instantly shot back in time to the underwater 25's we'd do on occasion. It involved pushing off the wall and kicking in streamline to the other end, staying under the surface the entire time. Sometimes we wore fins and other times we didn't. It was hard, to say the least.

During 4-7-8 breathing, my competitiveness switched on.

I remember hearing my "inner critic" tell me things like, "You better not breathe before she says you can," and "You were a swimmer; you should be the best at this!" I managed to hold my breath successfully, but my mind was full of judgment, comparison, and competition. These were only a few of the emotional and thought patterns that popped up.

This breathwork session, and the many that followed, showed me the power of intentional breath, or prana, which means breath *and* energy. Over the following many months, I showed up for myself with a daily breathwork practice, which helped me to bring past emotions, trauma, and stagnant energy to the surface to be released. Breathwork can be done on its own but is often associated with yoga (Kundalini, more specifically) and other meditation practices (all of which I recommend to my clients).

Another way to release your emotions is to get moving! Looking back at my time as a collegiate athlete, I realize I did this intuitively (and I'm not referring to the 20+ hours of swimming and dryland per week). Before every race, I would stand behind the block and shake out my hands and feet.

I never truly knew *why* I did this, but it made me feel a little less nervous. I now know that's **exactly** why. As I shook out my hands, I was shaking out and releasing my nervous energy. I could have very easily held this emotion, inadvertently making me more nervous. Yet, my body's wisdom told me otherwise. I had to shake it out to let it go. So, I did.

Whether in sport or life, you can use this technique to move the energy around and out! Get up. Shake out your hands, feet, or your entire body. Jump up and down. *Dance*, even. Put on your favorite song and dance around the room. Let your body flow to the music. Tune in and notice how your body *wants* to move out the energy. Your body holds innate wisdom and knows what it needs.

If dancing isn't your thing, get outside and go for a walk or jog. Pay close attention to how you feel as each foot hits the ground. Direct your attention to your surroundings. What do you see? What do you hear? Add in some handshaking during your walk.

When you return home, notice how the emotional energy has dissipated. Just like with anything, be consistent in this practice. The more awareness you bring to your emotions, the easier it will be to honor that feeling and recognize how your body wants to move the emotion out.

Finally, I want to provide insight around a holistic form of healing to release emotions from the body: Reiki Energy Healing. I went to a Reiki Master after experiencing chest pains for a week and walking myself to the emergency room. I spent five hours in the ER, and the doctors found no physiological explanation for this pain that I never experienced before, not even while swimming.

I felt hopeless when I left to go home. My godmother, Jennifer, recommended I make an appointment with a woman she had completed Reiki training alongside. I trust Jennifer and have always had faith in holistic practices (but had yet to try reiki), so I went.

Within five minutes of lying on the table, the Reiki Master (Alicia of Healing Spirit Café) told me my chakras were entirely blocked. A quick note for those who aren't familiar with the chakra system: The chakras are energy points that influence the body's mental and physical wellness of specific nerves, organs, and areas of the body.

When emotions are pushed down rather than fully felt, as is relevant to this book, the energy of the emotion may become trapped within the energetic body (or chakras). In time, this energy will negatively influence the mind, body, and soul. Reiki Energy Healing intends to move stuck energy out of the body, clearing the chakras and bringing the body and mind back into a state of balance.

During my first reiki treatment, Alicia told me that my chest pain might have reflected my solar plexus or heart chakra attempting to open while moving through many months of grief. At the time, I had been going to therapy and felt like I had made some breakthroughs, so this made sense. I had also been going to acupuncture once per week. I felt called to try more holistic forms of healing as the previous six months had been hell on Earth.

I had never been more stressed. I was still grieving the loss of my cousin. I felt like I was trudging through quicksand to make it to the end of my doctoral program. Let's not forget I had yet to work through ANY of my emotions around swimming, which had ended more than five years ago (at the time). To put it lightly—there was a **lot** to release.

Reiki, or universal life force energy, is a form of energy healing that aids in clearing out and balancing the energetic body. Originating in Japan, Reiki is a safe, non-intrusive hands-on technique used to treat physical, emotional, and spiritual ailments. Energy is all around us. You are made up of energy particles just like planets or stars. Even if you can't see energy, it is felt.

Have you ever been in the presence of someone who is filled with joy and excitement? How did you feel around them? Or imagine the opposite—what emotions came up in the presence of someone filled with hate or deep sadness? As a highly sensitive person, you likely felt what they felt in your mind, body, and soul. If you experienced their emotions and never released them, they may have become trapped within you, leading to physical symptoms.

Not only have you taken on the emotions of others, the energy and emotions attached to **your** emotions, past experiences, and conditioned beliefs must be expressed, too. Reiki is a healing modality that can help you move this energy out so it no longer affects you on a physical or emotional level.

Something I've learned since becoming a Reiki Level II Practitioner is that reiki energy will open the door for you to un-become all the conditioning that no longer serves you. It's a beautiful starting point for deconditioning, which is why I've incorporated reiki sessions into the Mind-Wise Method, my signature holistic wellness program for athletes and highly sensitive humans.

This program allows you to co-create a program unique to you and your life intentions. You have the option to combine Reiki, Human Design, and Mind-Wise Mentoring so you can release the emotions, beliefs, and past experiences that no longer serve you to make room for all that is meant for you in life after sport!

If you'd like to learn more, scan this QR code:

CHAPTER 9:

THE PROCESS OF UNBECOMING

On my journey, a word I've resonated deeply with is "unbecoming." Unbecoming is a process of recognizing and releasing all that you have been taught or experienced that no longer serves you. I began my process of unbecoming when I was 27 ½. My family experienced a horrific loss that led me to two choices: stay the same and suffer or choose change. I decided on Door Number Two.

After six months of talk therapy and close to a year of dance/movement therapy, I found myself thinking, "I'm doing great! I've done all the work and am healed." Oh boy, was I wrong. I had yet to do the deep work—the excavation of my trauma, loss, grief, fear, and shame. Although not all, much of this led me back to the pool. I learned how to recognize the deeply ingrained beliefs that continued to show up seven years after the fact.

Awareness is key. Once you are aware of something and how it affects you, you have the chance to choose change! I had to shine a light on the shadow—the parts of me I was afraid to bring to the surface. To quote my favorite fictional character, Professor Dumbledore, "Happiness can be found, even in the darkest of times, if one only remembers to turn on the light."

I did just that. While eternal happiness is never my goal (FYI, we aren't designed to be happy 24/7), I have un-become the conditioned beliefs, low vibration emotions (fear, grief, shame), and negative or traumatic experiences that no longer serve me. I made room for my true Self to shine.

There's always room for growth, and I continue to work on letting go of the beliefs and emotions that no longer serve me. The path to personal development and spiritual growth is a journey, not a destination.

Your true Self can shine, too, by bringing awareness to the conditioning you hold and releasing what no longer serves you. Throughout the unbecoming process, have self-compassion, grace, and patience. Take your time walking the path—your higher Self will be there waiting for you to arrive home.

Use the space below to begin your process of unbecoming (aka deconditioning). Write your conditioned beliefs in the left-hand column and identify what your true Self believes.

I recommend using this short Grounding Exercise (scan the QR code) before starting this activity, and it's never a bad idea to ask for support from a professional when you choose to decondition. This is *deep* work.

Example:

Conditioned Belief:
If I'm not doing the most,
I'm not doing enough.

True Self Belief:
It's okay to rest. In fact, rest is
essential to success.

Conditioned Belief:

True Self Belief:

_____   _____

_____   _____

Discovering Purpose After Sport

You may have felt your purpose was your sport throughout your athletic career or that your worth was dependent on your performance. I'm here to tell you that you were put on this earth for **so much more**. Even professional athletes may resonate with this, as you can only (physically and mentally) compete in your sport for so long.

At some point, you will move on. Then what? Your soul's purpose has been within you all along. You need only look inward to discover it!

To help facilitate your discovery, I use a tool called Human Design. We are all made up of energy—human design outlines how you are uniquely designed to exchange energy in this lifetime. A Human Design roadmap details the way to best use your energy to avoid burnout, how to make decisions that are energetically correct for you, and the difference between how you view yourself and how others perceive you. The roadmap allows you to find balance and harmony, eliminating resistance from your day-to-day.

In addition to human design, it's important you find stillness and silence if you want to uncover your true Self. In silence, you gain clarity and understanding around what you must accept or let go of. In stillness, you develop a deeper connection with yourself. The quieter you become, the more you can tune into what your body and soul call for in life after sport!

Doing this makes the process of unbecoming much easier as you will be able to clearly distinguish the conditioned beliefs taught to you by parents, coaches, and sport culture and the beliefs and values that come from within **you**. With this clarity, you can release what no longer serves you, including the stagnant energy or past experiences that got stuck in your body during the entirety of your athletic career. It's time you let go and made room for all that is *meant* for you.

We enter the world free of conditioning. If that's the case, though, why in the world am I sharing ways you can come home to your true Self as a highly sensitive athlete?

Picture this: A three-year-old child had to tag along to work with his mom, which happens to be a room full of college (women) athletes. The child sits at the front of the room drawing in his dragon coloring book while the team focuses on their sport psychology session. At one point or another, the boy gets hungry, so he is handed an apple by mom.

Without another thought, the young boy starts chomping down on his apple, happy as can be. Because why wouldn't he be? This boy didn't have any beliefs holding him back from enjoying his apple in the present moment. Not an ounce of embarrassment or self-consciousness (that I could tell)!

Now, flashback to me in ninth grade. I had a ham sandwich for lunch almost every day from elementary through high school. But, in ninth grade, I started doing the strangest thing. I found myself ripping up my sandwich into bite-sized pieces. I couldn't eat it whole.

Why? I was suddenly full of concern for the way I looked while eating my sandwich. I was hyper-aware of judgment, criticism, and embarrassment. My sensitivity was in hyperdrive at the lunch table, apparently, so I changed my behavior.

In all honesty, this made me feel even more uncomfortable. Why? Because my actions originated from the **fear** of rejection and judgment, rather than eating the damn sandwich whole—like I was meant to. I changed who I was to avoid ridicule from people who were more concerned with themselves anyway. I'd bet people didn't even notice me ripping up my sandwich because they were too absorbed by their own "stuff."

As we grow older and experience this (critical and harsh) world, there's a potential for closing off due to experiences of embarrassment, ridicule, shame, guilt, or fear. As I'm choosing to label it, this anxiety was a prime example of a shift from "confidence from within" to "validation from outside of self."

We develop this negative inner-critic in sport and life due to experience with expectations, comparison, and standards. This leads individuals (highly sensitive ones, particularly) to put on a mask to hide from the world. This behavior change (as displayed above) is exhausting.

If you want to embody your true Self, you must be willing to lean into failure, change, and even rejection. If you've lived your whole life up until this point based on what you've been told is "right" or how you "should" live, do, or be, then embodying who you are requires you to let go of all the **shoulds**. Stop "**should-ing**" all over yourself! The process of unbecoming and embodying invites you first to take a step back so that you can choose the path that's meant for you. It's your responsibility to un-learn the lessons that no longer serve you.

It's one thing to gain awareness of the embodiment process, and it's another thing to *live* it! It takes courage to release everything you've known despite also knowing it's not good for you.

To take the leap, you must have **faith**, trusting the Universe will support you. The Universe always has your best interest in mind, even if you can't envision the end result in that moment. Direct your attention to the joy of the process and release the need to have certainty about the outcome!

Daily Practice Fulfills Your Promise (to Yourself)

As an athlete, you know consistent practice is what led you to compete at the collegiate or even professional level. You didn't just wake up one day as a high-level athlete, as much as you might have wished it to come true! The same goes for letting go of past beliefs or stagnant emotions—you need to show up for yourself every day.

"*But I don't have time!*" Are you able to say positive affirmations as you look in the mirror while you brush your teeth? Can you put on a favorite song and dance around the kitchen while putting away the dishes?

What about taking five deep breaths in the shower, noticing how the hot water feels on your skin? Can you turn the TV off five minutes earlier than normal and grab your journal instead? These are all ways you can align with your soul's true design.

Stop getting in your way by saying you don't have time. It's up to **you** how you use your time. Pay attention to the "in-between" moments. You know, a couple of minutes in between work calls or classes or before practice. How can you move towards your most embodied Self during the "in-between?"

If you need the motivation to *take* the time to become your most authentic Self, think about your **why**. Why are you considering this change? How has wearing a mask for the last many years of your life affected you?

What are you missing out on because you've been worried about showing the world the real you? Or is it not about others but about not trusting **yourself** - not trusting that you can show up for and support yourself? Let's change that!

Rebuilding Self-Trust Through Consistent Routine

Throughout this book, we've talked about how, as a child, your highly sensitive Self felt less than, leading you to put on a mask and live outside of your comfort zone. You completely changed the way you showed up in the world because other people made you feel that being highly sensitive, introverted, or empathic was "too much." You might have been too much for *them*, but that doesn't mean *you* are too much for the world.

Your light is a gift to this world. By removing the mask, you reconnect with the child within you who was shamed for being sensitive. You have the opportunity to take this child by the hand and share the comfort, support, and kindness that they always gave to others but didn't often receive in return. You can shine a light on their superpowers and show them you can be trusted.

This inner trust is rebuilt every time you set a boundary and stick to it or each time you make a promise to yourself to dance to one song during the "in-between" moments throughout the day. It is within your control to rebuild trust within yourself and provide a secure home base for your true Self to shine.

This shining light brings an end to all the low vibrational energy holding you back; say goodbye to fear, guilt, and shame! "You have no home here," you can whisper (or shout) as those emotions are released from your mind and body. The more you show up for yourself, even in small or simple ways, the safer your true Self feels as it begins to show itself to the world around you.

CHAPTER 10:

EMBODYING THE MAGIC OF
YOUR TRUE SELF

Treat this final chapter like your personal journal. I've offered several embodiment practices that will help you release the conditioning you wrote about earlier and step into the **magic** of your true Self.

Use this section as you see fit. If the first practice that's calling to you is meditation, great! Sit for a meditation practice and write a few notes about what came up for you, how it felt, and why the practice is a good fit for you. Similarly, if "joyful movement" like yoga, dance, or hiking feels like a good place to start, amazing!

While you don't need to write things down each time, when you first implement these embodiment practices, I recommend putting pen to paper. This will enhance the lessons you take away from each experience and serve as beautiful reminders of your growth when you look back at the notes several months or even years from now.

If you would like additional support as you attempt to be consistent with your practices, don't hesitate to reach out to me via Instagram (@mindwisementor) or email (madeline@mindwisementor.com). In addition to mentoring, Energy Work and Human Design combined with your at-home practices will aid in the unbecoming and embodiment process. I would love to support you on your journey home to your true, sensitive Self. Below, your path home begins.

Balancing Your Energy
Your body is designed to live in harmony with itself and the world around it.

The body and soul crave balance, yet we are constantly allowing stress into our lives. This stress may come in many forms, such as pushing through pain, over-working, or never taking a rest day (or moment).

The key is to find the balance between always doing and simply being and between pushing towards your goals and choosing rest. Creating balance by dancing between the lines of structure, letting yourself flow from moment to moment. If you are **overly** structuring your life and not creating space for **flow**, your body will eventually give out.

For me, it was the chest pains I talked about early in this book. My body screamed, "**Enough!**" Learning to live in harmony with your true Self will lead to less resistance and more ease.

For this activity, use the space below to identify two things you can do that are grounding and structured and two things that are more restful and intuitive.

Here's an example: I will commit to one yoga class a week at 6 pm on Mondays. (Remember, this has two aspects of structure—Mondays at 6 pm and once per week, plus yoga, which enhances present moment, body awareness/intuition.)

I will also have a five-minute afternoon dance party on weekdays (five minutes on weekdays is the structure, while dancing is more flowy and in the moment).

Your turn!

_____

_____

_____

_____

_____

Meditation: Mindfulness and Manifestation

Have you tried meditation before? There are many forms, but these are the two I'm recommending as you work towards stepping into your true Self. The first is mindfulness meditation, which typically involves sitting with a straight, yet soft, spine and focusing your attention on the breath.

You can use a phone app (I recommend 10% Happier or Headspace) or find a meditation on YouTube. Either way, the intention of this meditation is not to clear the mind. Rather, you are invited to **notice** when your attention has wandered, possibly becoming swept up by a thought, memory, or outside sound.

The moment you notice your mind has wandered, simply begin again by coming back to the breath. You may have to begin again many times, and that's okay. That is the practice. You are strengthening your mindfulness muscle, just like you strengthened your physical body or sharpened your sport skills as an athlete.

This practice will help you become more grounded and aware of your thoughts, a skill that will benefit you in all aspects of life. You will become more attuned to the subtleties of your inner world, recognizing negative thought patterns or conditioned beliefs that no longer serve you. With this awareness, it becomes easier to let them go.

My suggestion is to start small with a five-minute meditation. Bring a beginner's mind to this practice. Don't attempt to rush ahead or judge yourself when your mind wanders. This does **not** make you a "bad" meditator. The fact that you even noticed your mind was wandering indicates the *opposite*!

Remind yourself of the very first practice you ever attended. Were you an expert on that day? I know I wasn't! I couldn't even put the arms and legs together for the butterfly on my first day. I ended up going to the National Championships to swim butterfly ten years later. Don't give up; try, try again!

Use this space to write about your experience meditating every day for a week. Did you notice any emotions? Specific thoughts or conditioned beliefs? Did any particular experiences come to mind?

_____

_____

_____

_____

_____

Another form of meditation that will benefit you on your path to self-discovery is manifestation visualization. Again, you can find this on many meditation apps (I like "Insight Timer") or YouTube. This form of visualization allows you to use your inner vision to clearly see, feel, hear, and **become** your true Self.

Sink into the way your true Self acts, thinks, talks, dresses, feels, and lives. Rather than wanting this vision to "come true," remind yourself that this is **already within you**. Your Highest Self is the highest energy and potential of **you**. The more often you embody the real you in your mind's eye, the easier it will be to embody your Highest Self in your day-to-day. Claim this image as your reality, and begin living in alignment!

Reflection: Describe what you saw in your visualization. Putting it down on paper helps to make it more tangible. Detail how you felt, dressed, acted, worked, loved, and moved.

What can you do *today* to move 1% closer to embodying this vision?

Breathwork

Establishing a breathwork practice marked a pivotal point in my healing journey. Tuning into my breath helped me slow down my overactive mind and reconnect with my body. It was there that the energy of repressed emotions and conditioned beliefs remained.

It was in my body, not my mind, that I had the opportunity to honor all that **was** and let it go to make room for all that's **meant** to be. The process of unbecoming doesn't occur in the mind; remember, emotions are felt in the **body**.

Breathwork is such a powerful tool. When you focus on an extended exhale (or letting go), your body responds by softening, slowing down, and relaxing. The exhale releases you from a state of survival (fight or flight) and gently guides you to a state of "rest and digest." It's in this state that you can tune into the true needs of your body. In the silence, you can hear what your body is calling for.

Similar to crying, the exhale is a form of expression and release. When you practice breathwork, you may notice thoughts, memories, feelings, or energy bubble to the surface—breathwork helps make the unconscious conscious!

I recommend starting this practice using a simple technique and building upon it with time. You will also benefit greatly from the support of a professional trained in breathwork. I'll provide links to breathwork groups and practitioners in the Resources section. For now, start here and take time to reflect on the experience:

Settle into a comfortable position with a straight, yet relaxed, spine.

Gently place your hands, palms facing down, on your knees. Sit here for a moment and settle into stillness, breathing normally. When you feel grounded, you can close your eyes (if you feel comfortable) and begin this sequence:

Breathe in deeply through your nose for 1, 2, 3, 4 (seconds).

Hold the breath at the top for 1, 2, 3, 4, 5, 6, 7.

Exhale slow and controlled through the mouth for 1, 2, 3, 4, 5, 6, 7, 8.

Repeat (3-5x).

After your final round, remain seated with eyes open or closed and breathe normally for a minute or so. Just breathe. Just be. When you feel ready, come back to this section and spend a few minutes reflecting on the experience.

Like any practice, I suggest you set a goal for the number of times you will sit for breathwork each week. What feels realistic and supportive for you? From start to finish, this practice will take no more than 10 minutes. How many times per week will you commit to 10 minutes of breathwork and reflection? You can write this goal below, alongside your reflection of the experience.

How did it feel in your mind? In your body? What came up for you, if anything?

_____

_____

_____

_____

_____

Self-Alignment Affirmations

"I am strong. I am courageous. I am bold. I am abundant. I am fearless. I am loved. I am *sensitive*."

You've been told again and again how you **should** be. It's time you took your power back! Who *are* you at *this* moment? How do you want to show up? Can you reframe the way you speak to yourself and begin living in alignment with an abundance mindset?

If you've been so focused on all the things you don't have or feel you **should** be ("Why can't I be less sensitive? I don't want to be so _____. Why should I even bother, I'll never have ____."), you're missing out on all that's **meant for you**. Choose to shift your language to reflect your true Self!

Below, write a list of all that you *are*. If they aren't all "I am" statements, that's okay—don't get stuck on the need to begin with "I am." The most important aspect of this exercise is to phrase it in the **present tense** versus past or future. Refer back to your list of strengths, values, and aspects of your true identity. How do you want to show up each day?

I am _____

I am _____

I am _____

I am _____

I am _____

I am _____

I am _____

Once you have your list, pick three each day to repeat to yourself first thing in the morning. If you already have a morning routine, great! Add your three affirmations to this practice. Consider repeating these statements to yourself while brushing your teeth or taking a shower.

The easiest way to establish a new habit or routine is to add to something you're already doing. Keep it simple! When you feel ready, you can take it up a notch and repeat these in the mirror while making eye contact with yourself. Your true Self wants to be *seen*. Let it shine by giving yourself the energy and attention you deserve!

Joyful Movement

Meditation, breathwork, and affirmations involve getting grounded and finding stillness or silence so you can access all that's meant for you. This next practice consists of the opposite! As an athlete, I hope that you enjoyed your sport at one point or another. I used to **love** to swim. It brought me so much joy for many years.

At a certain point, though, my body no longer liked the repetition of thousands of yards up and down the lanes in combination with dry land exercises, such as lifting (heavy-ish) weights and high-intensity or explosive movements. In college, I found myself with a "swimmer's shoulder." It was clear that my body no longer responded positively to this form of training.

For two years following the end of my swimming career, I said "hell no!" to high-intensity, structured workouts. It felt like I had developed a negative relationship or belief around this form of structured exercise because of the negative energy I continued to hold from losing my sport.

After two years of inactivity (besides walking the dog and going to and from school), I had gained nearly 30 pounds and felt downright awful. When I looked in the mirror, I barely recognized the reflection staring back at me. At the time, I thought I wanted my "swimmer's body" back. I realized I had to let that picture of myself go because who I was **now** was not the same person that I was then.

I began my fitness journey, determined to lose weight. I tried several different exercise programs, joined several gyms, yet nothing stuck. I would eventually lose motivation and stop going altogether, even if it meant losing money for canceling my reservation late. I always ended up in a shame spiral for not wanting to show up to the class. Why wasn't anything sticking? I was an athlete. I know how to work out, and I've trained hard before, so what was going on?

After five failed attempts at sticking to a workout class or specific gym, I made a realization: I didn't actually **enjoy** anything I had tried. Except for a kickboxing gym which ended up being my longest membership at eight or so months, the rest died off within one or two. Yet, the kickboxing gym didn't work out in the end, either. I started strong and was going to two classes per week (sometimes three) and then found myself becoming less and less motivated. In this case, it was less the exercise itself and more the environment.

Another realization I came to was that I don't enjoy exercising in big groups or going to a gym for a class. I enjoy working out at home or outside! "But you were on a team for 14 years? How did you manage for so long if you really don't like it?"

The water was my saving grace. At swim practice, I could put my head down in the water, and the world around me became quiet. It was just me and the black line at the bottom of the pool. I was in my own bubble, my own energy, until I reached the wall. The water supported my high sensitivity, as well. The water dimmed the bright lights, muffled the loud cheers, and lessened the harsh feedback of the scoreboard and time clock.

I must take a moment to express my gratitude. Every pool I swam in felt equally supportive because they all had one thing in common: the element of water. The water cooled the fire that burned within me—the intensity and stimulation of the world.

So, what's the point of this story? As a highly sensitive athlete, you need to tune into how your body *wants* to move and *where* you feel best doing it. Outside of your sport, have you ever taken the time to consider what form of movement makes you feel most in alignment with your true Self?

Nowadays, I most prefer walking outside and have stuck to a weekly yoga practice for the last five months! I've also made a promise to myself to lift my at-home weights two times a week and to stop referring to them as "baby weights." The language we choose can significantly affect us, and I want to feel strong and powerful. I choose to tune into how my body feels each time I pick them up and put them down, whether they are eight pounds or 25 pounds.

Use the space below to consider the different forms of exercise and movement **your** body enjoys. Nothing is too small. Consider things like dancing around your living room to your favorite playlist, gardening, hiking, stretching, walking to and from work or school (rather than sitting on the subway or stuck in traffic), or anything else you feel called to engage in!

What are your forms of joyful movement?

_____

_____

_____

_____

_____

Shake It Out!

The final embodiment practice I'd like to offer you is to **shake it out**! That's literally it—just shake! When you notice yourself feeling an onset of emotion or intense energy, choose a way to physically *release* it.

My favorite way is through shaking out the hands, feet, or entire body—whatever feels most supportive for you! There are no rules here. Let it out. Shake out your face, too; make it silly and playful.

Let yourself laugh if that feels right. You may feel the need to cry or let out a deep sigh. Whatever comes up for you is right for you. Do this often—the more, the better.

As a highly sensitive human, you are constantly taking in energy in all forms. While some of this energy will make you feel good, plenty of the energy isn't yours to hold. Let that shiz go and shake it out!

Use the space below to reflect on how you feel any time you do this, and use this as a reminder for **why** you can choose this strategy. In short, shaking off the energy that doesn't serve you is a fast-track to **unbecoming!**

How do you feel after shaking it out?

_____

_____

_____

_____

_____

In addition to the embodiment practices detailed above, I recommend yoga (any form that calls to you, including Kundalini Yoga, which is focused on breathwork and mantra practices), Tai Chi or Qi Gong, Reiki healing, acupuncture, bodywork such as massage, and ecstatic (free form) dance. Most importantly, choose what calls to you and build a community if you can! As an athlete, this sense of community allowed you to deepen your training and feel a sense of connection. The same can be said for finding a spiritual or movement-based community in life after sport!

CONCLUSION:

A STANDING OVATION (FOR YOU)

As you come to the end of this book, take a moment to celebrate the steps you've taken thus far to begin embodying your true Self—your most magical, sensitive Self. Take back your power, and ignite your true fire within. You are shamelessly sensitive. You are magic. Rise into the power of your sensitive traits, and let your light shine!

As you continue on your journey inward, choose support and community as you make your way through the darkness. To truly experience the light, you must walk through the dark. As a highly sensitive athlete, you have either turned your head to the dark or have greeted it like an old friend. As you move forward in sport and life, walk courageously through the dark, letting go of any fear, shame, or guilt.

When you choose to put yourself first and live each day with authenticity, your energy will spill over and lift up those around you! You can put yourself first *and* care deeply for others. Take your time uncovering the layers of yourself you have covered up for so long.

Your life isn't a race. You aren't behind, and there's no rush. You are right where you're meant to be. When you're ready, remove the mask you have worn for far too long and step into your true **magic**. The world needs your light. Let it shine far and bright. You have all you need within you.

RESOURCES

The Mind-Wise Method, Human Design Roadmap & Reading, or Energy Healing with Madeline: mindwisementor.com

Athletes Soul

Dayluna Human Design Podcast

Genius Bahar (@geniusbahar): Reiki Master Teacher

10% Happier App and Podcast

Headspace Meditation App

Healing Spirit Café/Alicia Phillips: Reiki Master Teacher

Her Beyond Sports Story (@hersportsstory)

The Hidden Opponent

Highly Sensitive Refuge

MyHuddle

Insight Timer App

Natalie Saimeri (@theemotionsqueen): Emotional Healing through Somatic Work, Meditation & Breathwork

Nina Rizzo (@iamninafrancis): Yoga & Meditation Teacher

Sarah Wingert (@wildlyradiantwoman): School of Radiance

Shannon Dolan (@healthwithshannon): Feminine Vitality Online Course

The Virago Project

The Well Studio with Marissa Nash: Yoga, Meditation, and Community

NOTES

REFERENCES

Aron, E. N. The Highly Sensitive Person: How to Thrive When the World Overwhelms You. New York: Birch Lane Press, 1996.

Aron, E. (2021). The highly sensitive person. Hsperson.com

Arvinen-Barrow, Hurley, & Ruiz. (2017). Transitioning out of professional sport: The psychosocial career-ending injuries among elite Irish rugby football. Journal of Clinical Sport Psychology, 11(1), 67-84.

Barlow, M. (2019). Reframe, regroup, refresh: Navigating the transition from athlete to exerciser. Proquest, 1-114.

Barlow, M., Warner, S., & Sachs, M. (2018). Life after collegiate sport: From athlete to exerciser. Paper presented at the Association for Applied Sport Psychology Conference, Toronto, ON.

Benham, G. (2006). The highly sensitive person: Stress and physical symptom reports. Personality and Individual Differences, 40, 1433-1440.

Boyer, A. (2021, January 27). The difference between hypersensitivity and high sensitivity. https://highlysensitiverefuge.com/hypersensitivity-high-sensitivity/

Cain, S. Quiet: The Power of Introverts in a World That Can't Stop Talking. New York: Crown Publishers, 2012.

Cassil, A. The empowered highly sensitive person: A workbook to harness your strengths in every part of life.

Dyer, N. L., Baldwin, A. L., & Rand, W. L. (2019). A large-scale effectiveness trial of reiki for physical and psychological health. The Journal of Alternative and Complementary Medicine, 25(12), 1156-1162.

Grove, J. R., Lavallee, D., & Gordon, S. (1997). Coping with retirement from sport: The influence of athletic identity. Journal of Applied Sport Psychology, 9, 191-203.

Haelle, T. (2018, April 18). The consequences of compensation in autism. Neurology Advisor. https://www.neurologyadvisor.com/topics/autism-spectrum-disorder/the-consequences-of-compensation-in-autism/

Hendriksen, E. How to Be Yourself: Quiet your inner critic and rise above social anxiety. New York: St. Martin's Press, 2018.

Hu, R. U., & Bunnell, L. (2011). The definitive book of human design: The science of differentiation. HDC Publishing.

Johnston, J., Harwood, C., & Minniti, A. M. (2013). Positive youth development in swimming: Clarification and consensus of key psychosocial assets. Journal of Applied Sport Psychology, 25, 392-411.

Marcia, J. E. (1966). Development and validation of ego-identity status. Journal of Personality and Social Psychology, 3(5), 551-558.

McGonigal, K. The joy of movement: How exercise helps us find happiness, hope, connection, and courage. New York: Avery, 2019.

Miles, P., & True, G. (2003). Reiki—Review of a biofield therapy. History, theory, practice, and research. Alternative Therapies, 9(2),62-72.

Mitchell, T. O., Nesti, M., Richardson, D., Midgley, A. W., Eubank, M., & Littlewood, M. (2014). Exploring athletic identity in elite-level English youth football: A cross-sectional approach. Journal of Sports Sciences, 32(13), 1294-1299.

Muscara, C. Stop missing your life: How to be deeply present in an un-present world. New York: Hachette Books, 2019.

Quest, P. Reiki for Life: The Complete Guide to Reiki Practice for Level 1, 2, & 3. New York: Tarcher and Perigee, 2016.

Tucker, I. (2012, March 31). Susan Cain: 'Society has a cultural bias towards extroverts.' The Guardian. https://www.theguardian.com/technology/2012/apr/01/susan-cain-extrovert-introvert-interview

Van der Kolk, B. The Body Keeps the Score: Brain, Mind, and Body in the Healing of Trauma. New York: Penguin, 2014.

Vitale, A. (2007). An integrative review of reiki touch therapy research. Holistic Nursing Practice, 21(4), 167-179.

.

Made in the USA
Las Vegas, NV
13 October 2024

96761275R00056